HIDDEN HAZARDS OF ONLINE ADVERTISING

AN INVESTIGATION OF CONSUMER SECURITY AND DATA PRIVACY ISSUES

INTERNET POLICIES AND ISSUES

Additional books in this series can be found on Nova's website
under the Series tab.

Additional e-books in this series can be found on Nova's website
under the e-book tab.

INTERNET POLICIES AND ISSUES

HIDDEN HAZARDS OF ONLINE ADVERTISING

AN INVESTIGATION OF CONSUMER SECURITY AND DATA PRIVACY ISSUES

LILLIAN WALLACE
EDITOR

New York

NOTICE TO THE READER

LIBRARY OF CONGRESS CATALOGING-IN-PUBLICATION DATA

ISBN: 978-1-63321-458-3

Published by Nova Science Publishers, Inc. † New York

Contents

PREFACE

Chapter 1 - In this chapter, the Permanent Subcommittee on Investigations of the U.S. Senate Homeland Security and Governmental Affairs Committee examined issues of consumer privacy and security on the Internet and in the broader online economy. Central to this segment of the economy is the online advertising industry, which continues to grow in importance. In 2013, U.S. online advertising revenue for the first time surpassed that of broadcast television advertising as companies spent nearly $43 billion to reach consumers.

The online advertising ecosystem is highly complex. Online advertisers do far more than merely disseminate text, graphic, or video advertisements. Underlying the work of online advertisers are sophisticated systems that are able to identify and target specific consumer groups with relevant advertising, as well as state-of-the art security practices to monitor the integrity of these ad delivery systems. The ability to target advertising is a key function of online ad delivery systems, and advertisers are willing to pay a premium of between 60 and 200 percent for these services. With the continuing boom in mobile devices, the importance, and complexity, of digital advertising is likely to continue increasing in years to come.

The Subcommittee's investigation focused on the features and vulnerabilities in the online advertising industry that invite malware attacks. The Subcommittee also sought to highlight the potential hazards to private consumer information which result from consumer visits to even mainstream websites. The Subcommittee surveyed Internet participants and interviewed representatives from major ad networks, ad exchanges, data brokers, self-regulatory bodies, the Federal Trade Commission, consumer protection groups, and other participants in the online advertising industry to identify the vulnerabilities that have led to significant hazards to consumer safety and loss of consumer privacy online.

Chapter 2 – This is the Testimony of Alex Stamos, Vice President of Information Security, Yahoo! Inc. Hearing on "Online Advertising and Hidden Hazards to Consumer Security and Data Privacy."

Chapter 3 - This is the Testimony of George Salem, Senior Product Manager, Google, Inc. Hearing on "Online Advertising and Hidden Hazards to Consumer Security and Data Privacy."

Chapter 4 – This is the Statement of Craig D. Spiezle, Executive Director and President, Online Trust Alliance. Hearing on "Online Advertising and Hidden Hazards to Consumer Security and Data Privacy."

Chapter 5 – This is the Statement of Maneesha Mithal, Associate Director, Division of Privacy and Identity Protection, Federal Trade Commission. Hearing on "Online Advertising and Hidden Hazards to Consumer Security and Data Privacy."

Chapter 6 – This is the Testimony of Luigi Mastria, Executive Director, Digital Advertising Alliance. Hearing on "Online Advertising and Hidden Hazards to Consumer Security and Data Privacy."

In: Hidden Hazards of Online Advertising   ISBN: 978-1-63321-458-3
Editor: Lillian Wallace   © 2014 Nova Science Publishers, Inc.

Chapter 1

ONLINE ADVERTISING AND HIDDEN HAZARDS TO CONSUMER SECURITY AND DATA PRIVACY[*]

Senate Permanent Subcommittee on Investigations

I. EXECUTIVE SUMMARY

For the past year, the Permanent Subcommittee on Investigations of the U.S. Senate Homeland Security and Governmental Affairs Committee has been examining issues central to consumer privacy and security on the Internet and in the broader online economy. Central to this segment of the economy is the online advertising industry, which continues to grow in importance. In 2013, U.S. online advertising revenue for the first time surpassed that of broadcast television advertising as companies spent $42.8 billion to reach consumers.[1]

The online advertising ecosystem is highly complex. Online advertisers do far more than merely disseminate text, graphic, or video advertisements. Underlying the work of online advertisers are sophisticated systems that are able to identify and target specific consumer groups with relevant advertising, as well as state-of-the art security practices to monitor the integrity of these ad delivery systems. The ability to target advertising is a key function of online ad delivery systems, and advertisers are willing to pay a premium of between

---

[*] This is an edited, reformatted and augmented version of a staff report released May 15, 2014.

60 and 200 percent for these services.[2] With the continuing boom in mobile devices, the importance, and complexity, of digital advertising is likely to continue increasing in years to come.[3]

Although consumers are becoming increasingly vigilant about safeguarding the information they share on the Internet, many are less informed about the plethora of information created about them by online companies as they travel the Internet. A consumer may be aware, for example, that a search engine provider may use the search terms the consumer enters in order to select an advertisement targeted to his interests. Consumers are less aware, however, of the true scale of the data being collected about their online activity. A visit to an online news site may trigger interactions with hundreds of other parties that may be collecting information on the consumer as he travels the web. The Subcommittee found, for example, a trip to a popular tabloid news website triggered a user interaction with some 352 other web servers as well. Many of those interactions were benign; some of those third-parties, however, may have been using cookies or other technology to compile data on the consumer. The sheer volume of such activity makes it difficult for even the most vigilant consumer to control the data being collected or protect against its malicious use.

Furthermore, the growth of online advertising has brought with it a rise in cybercriminals attempting to seek out and exploit weaknesses in the ecosystem and locate new potential victims. Many consumers are unaware that mainstream websites are becoming frequent avenues for cybercriminals seeking to infect a consumer's computer with advertisement-based malware, or "malvertising." Some estimates state that malvertising has increased over 200% in 2013 to over 209,000 incidents generating over 12.4 billion malicious ad impressions.[4] According to a recent study by the security firm Symantec, more than half of Internet website publishers have suffered a malware attack through a malicious advertisement.[5]

The Subcommittee seeks to highlight this specific aspect of online security. The Internet as a whole, as well as all the consumers who visit mainstream websites, is vulnerable to the growing number of malware attacks through online advertising. While there are many other significant vulnerabilities on the Internet, malware attacks delivered through online advertising are a real and growing problem.

The complexity of the online advertising industry makes it difficult to identify and hold accountable the entities responsible for damages resulting from malware attacks. Those attempting to exploit the Internet for criminal purposes are certainly the most culpable, and ensuring the government has adequate criminal enforcement authority is critical to deterring this activity. Yet, if responsibility for malware attacks is laid solely on cybercriminals, commercial actors may have reduced incentives to develop and institute security measures for fear of becoming the liable party if something goes wrong. The Subcommittee's investigation shows that lack of accountability within the online advertising industry may lead to overly lax security regimes, creating serious vulnerabilities for Internet users. Such vulnerabilities could grow worse in the absence of additional incentives for the most capable parties on the Internet to work with consumers and other stake holders to take effective precautionary measures.

a. Subcommittee Investigation

With this investigation the Subcommittee seeks to highlight malvertising, a growing threat to consumers and the online industry. The threat malware poses to consumers is not new, and the sources of malware and the vulnerabilities it exploits are often well documented. Malware can exploit malicious code in pirated software,[6] or vulnerabilities in mainstream software and operating systems. Although malware is most commonly hosted on websites with little or no security oversight, or even completely fraudulent websites visited by consumers, each year more consumers are delivered malware through mainstream websites that may have been compromised or are unwittingly serving malicious advertising.[7]

Several legislative proposals to strengthen Internet privacy and security have stalled, and there currently is no sector-specific federal data privacy law for Internet companies.[8] Self- regulatory standards set by the online industry, while having significant privacy guidance, do not outline comprehensive security standards. Furthermore, the FTC has brought no cases related to malware transmitted through advertisements, and has not issued comprehensive regulations to curb deceptive or unfair practices in online advertising, including setting minimum safeguards on consumer data collection practices or establishing liability for damages caused by advertisements that transmit malware attacks on Internet users.[9] To address privacy issues in online advertising, in February 2012, President Obama urged the industry to implement a "Do Not Track" button that would allow users to control the extent to which they are tracked on the Internet for online advertising purposes.[10] However, the Do Not Track initiative has stalled, with advertisers and consumer groups unable to agree on even a definition of what constitutes "tracking."[11]

The Subcommittee conducted an investigation focusing specifically on the features and vulnerabilities in the online advertising industry that invite malware attacks. The Subcommittee also sought to highlight the potential hazards to private consumer information which result from consumer visits to even mainstream websites. The Subcommittee surveyed Internet participants and interviewed representatives from major ad networks, ad exchanges, data brokers, self- regulatory bodies, the Federal Trade Commission, consumer protection groups, and other participants in the online advertising industry to identify the vulnerabilities that have led to significant hazards to consumer safety and loss of consumer privacy online. Every entity contacted by the Subcommittee cooperated with requests for information.

b. Investigation Overview

In December 2013, an Internet user visited a popular, mainstream website. Without any further action on her part, her computer was infected with a virus: all the personal information, usernames, and passwords she used on her device could have been stolen, and her computer hijacked.[12] The owners of the website she visited had no idea that the attack had taken place because the virus came not from the website itself, but from an embedded online advertisement managed by the Internet company Yahoo's online advertising network.[13] The user did not need to click on the advertisement—indeed, if the mainstream website she visited had time to load onto her computer before the malware was delivered, the frame where the advertisement would have gone would have been empty because the cybercriminals didn't even bother putting an image in.[14] The owners of the website where the advertisement ran did not even know who had delivered the malware because, in today's complex online advertising industry, websites often have no direct relationship with the entities that advertise on their sites. Although Yahoo reacted promptly to the attack, as many as 2 million consumers may have been exposed to the covert advertising malware.[15]

In February 2014, cybercriminals launched a similar attack on YouTube through an advertisement delivered by Google.[16] As in the Yahoo attack, the user did not need to click on the advertisement in question.[17] Google also responded quickly to that attack. Similar attacks have struck across many online advertising platforms.

As it turned out, in the December 2013 attack, Yahoo's network was compromised by a hacker who had stolen a Yahoo employee's credentials, not through any structural weakness unique to Yahoo. But cybercriminals have numerous methods to evade security measures. For example, cybercriminals time their attacks carefully, often picking U.S. holidays or Friday afternoons when they believe online traffic will be high and there will be fewer security personnel available to react. The practice is so pervasive that when law enforcement personnel raid cyber-criminal residences and offices in Russia and other foreign countries, they find calendars extensively marked with U.S. federal holidays and three-day weekends.

These incidents demonstrated the importance of educating the public on the threat of malvertising. The Subcommittee discovered no evidence to suggest Google or Yahoo's ad network is any more vulnerable to malware attacks than any other major online ad network. Yahoo and Google appear to follow standard industry practice. However, the industry as a whole remains vulnerable to these forms of attack.

The prevalence of vulnerabilities in the online advertising industry has made it difficult for individual industry participants to adopt effective long-term security countermeasures. Many entities use "scanning" to search for malicious advertisements, an automated process that mimics loading each advertisement onto a webpage on test machines to see if malware is transmitted. However, this scanning is rendered increasingly ineffective by cybercriminals who endeavor to, in essence, learn the geographic location of the scanners and then direct malicious advertisements away from those scanners. In other instances, cybercriminals change the nature of an advertisement after it has been scanned and cleared, turning an initially benign advertisement into malware.

Beyond scanning, most protective measures for consumers and their data come from industry-led voluntary compliance regimes and the contractual relationships between entities in the advertising ecosystem. But those voluntary compliance regimes and contractual arrangements are often incomplete, unreliable, or poorly enforced. As the online advertising industry grows increasingly complex, it is also becoming more difficult to ascertain responsibility when consumers are hurt by malicious advertising or data collection.

A cautious citizen can avoid becoming a victim of crime in real life by, for example, avoiding bad neighborhoods and keeping a wary eye on the street traffic. But, online, a visit to even a reputable website can now result in thousands of dollars in damage to the consumer and the compromise of private information at the hands of actors most consumers don't know are present.

Vulnerabilities in online advertising stem from the fact that advertisements online differ in nature from advertisements broadcast on radio or television. On radio or television, the content of the advertisement is transmitted by the same party that hosts the rest of the content on the station. A radio station, for example, may play a recording of an advertisement on the same frequency and equipment it uses for playing songs. A television station may broadcast commercials from the same studio that is transmitting the evening news. By contrast, if a user visits a mainstream website, the server that hosts the website is often not the server that selects and delivers an advertisement that runs on the website.

Host websites most commonly sell ad space on their sites through an intermediary, most often an ad platform operated by well-known tech companies.[18] These intermediary companies manage "real estate" on the host websites, filling the spaces set aside by the host with advertisements. These intermediary companies also typically gather data on Internet users for the purpose of individually targeting online advertisements to those users when they visit partner websites. Through a complicated series of Internet transactions, the intermediary companies— often referred to as ad networks or exchanges—ultimately direct an Internet user's browser to display an advertisement from a server controlled by neither the ad network nor the original host website.

Separating the party who delivers the online advertisement from the party who runs the host website means that the consumer who visits the host website is forced to trust her data and security to a party unknown to her. While a consumer might think visiting an online news site is safe because of the mainstream trustworthiness of the entity, the consumer's computer and personal information are actually at the mercy of dozens, or even hundreds, of other businesses and individuals that such websites may not even be aware of or have a direct relationship with.

The Subcommittee's investigation has revealed that host websites often do not select and cannot predict which advertisements will be delivered by the intermediary ad networks that rent space on their websites. They may not know what entities are running advertisements on their site until they receive feedback from ad networks after the fact. In fact, many host websites rely on ad networks, exchanges, supply-side platforms (SSPs) and demand-side platforms (DSPs) to handle security and quality control.

In some cases, host websites are not consulted about what kind of cookies are used, what types of consumer data are being collected, or what vulnerabilities for malicious software are contained in the advertisements being run on their websites.

Today, most ad networks and exchanges also have limited control over the actual content of the advertisements whose placement they facilitate. While many do robust scanning to detect malware, the ad networks and exchanges do not control the server that ultimately delivers the advertisement to the host website. Sometimes, a malicious advertiser will initially appear benign, but change its advertisement once it has passed through initial scans. On other occasions, a malicious party will infiltrate the ad network itself and pass malware on to unsuspecting consumers.

Despite the difficulty in eliminating bad actors from the online advertising ecosystem, ad networks are currently engaged in multiple industry-led efforts to set best practices guidelines.

While the ad networks uniformly force advertisers to agree to follow codes of conduct drawn up by voluntary self-regulatory agencies like the Network Advertising Initiative (NAI) or the Digital Advertising Alliance (DAA), the scope of the codes of conduct and the oversight of company compliance with these standards can be limited. For example, NAI has just seven employees reviewing or auditing 91 companies.[19] The codes themselves are predominantly oriented toward privacy concerns, and do not comprehensively address online advertising malware security.

The complex interactions underlying the online advertising industry that make it vulnerable to malware attacks also underscore the difficulties in enforcing restrictions on the collection and use of sensitive consumer data. Multiple companies told the Subcommittee that, while they do scan for malware, there is no scanning or automated process in place to check for compliance on the part of advertisers who limit the operation of cookies used to collect consumer data. While self-regulatory codes or particular contracts might require advertisers or ad networks to limit their collection of consumer data to non-personally identifiable information (non-PII), there is little systematic oversight to ensure that practice conforms to the contractual obligations.

Self-regulation in the online advertising industry has worked in some areas, but needs strengthening in some key respects. On the privacy side, self-regulatory groups such as the DAA and NAI have created guidelines and standards widely adopted by online advertising companies. Detection of deviation of those standards and punishment for noncompliance has sometimes been weak, as examples in this report indicate, but there are enforcement mechanisms that do hold companies accountable in some cases. Comparable standards and enforcement mechanisms have not materialized for online advertising security, however.

A new industry effort to address fraudulent advertising called Trust in Ads was launched on May 8, 2014.[20] While the existence of such an effort is a positive development, further efforts to create real self-regulation on security in online advertising will be needed to make meaningful progress.

At this time, government rules regarding online advertising also fail to comprehensively safeguard consumers or level the playing field for companies working to prevent advertising malware. The Federal Trade Commission (FTC), the key government agency overseeing online activities, has brought over 100 enforcement actions related to online data privacy and security problems. However, most of the FTC's online enforcement actions have been brought under the auspices of statutes prohibiting companies from engaging in "deceptive" practices, although the FTC also has enforcement authority to stop "unfair" practices.[21] In deceptive practice cases, a company typically has made a specific promise not to engage in a particular practice, but does so anyway. Such cases, while egregious, can only be brought when a company makes a specific representation and then fails to follow it. While the FTC has brought cases against some companies under its authority to regulate "unfair" practices, industry participants claim not to have a clear understanding of what practices are actually forbidden.[22] In addition, although the FTC has pursued Internet security cases, those cases have focused primarily on improper storage of personal information. Congress has not passed legislation on this topic, and the FTC has brought no cases related to malware transmitted through advertisements, and has not issued comprehensive regulations to curb deceptive or unfair practices in online advertising, including setting minimum safeguards on consumer data collection practices or establishing liability for damages caused by advertisements that transmit malware attacks on Internet users.[23]

The online advertising industry can be complex and difficult to understand. In such an environment, determining responsible parties when things go wrong can be difficult. What is clear, however, is that the one party who is least capable of monitoring and regulating advertising—the consumer—is the party who currently bears the full brunt of the losses when the system fails.

c. Findings and Recommendations

Findings

Based on the Subcommittee's investigation, the Report makes the following findings of fact.

1. **Consumers risk exposure to malware through everyday activity.** Consumers can incur malware attacks without having taken any action other than visiting a mainstream website. The complexity of the online advertising ecosystem makes it impossible for an ordinary consumer to avoid advertising malware attacks, identify the source of the malware exposure, and determine whether the ad network or host website could have prevented the attack.

2. **The complexity of current online advertising practices impedes industry accountability for malware attacks.** The online advertising industry has grown in complexity to such an extent that each party can conceivably claim it is not responsible when malware is delivered to a user's computer through an advertisement. An ordinary online advertisement typically goes through five or six intermediaries before being delivered to a user's browser, and the ad networks themselves rarely deliver the actual advertisement from their own servers. In most cases, the owners of the host website visited by a user do not know what advertisements will be shown on their site.

3. **Self-regulatory bodies alone have not been adequate to ensure consumer security online.** Self-regulatory codes of conduct in the online advertising field do not comprehensively address consumer security from malware. In addition, the self-regulatory efforts in online security to date have been dependent upon online ad networks for their funding and viability, creating a potential conflict of interest in their dual roles as industry advocates and standard-setting bodies. The self-regulatory bodies prioritize industry representatives over consumer advocates in the standard-setting process.

4. **Visits to mainstream websites can expose consumers to hundreds of unknown, or potentially dangerous, third parties.** Subcommittee analysis of several popular websites found that visiting even a mainstream website exposes consumers to hundreds of third parties. Each of those third parties may be capable of collecting information on the consumer and, in extreme scenarios, is a potential source of malware.

5. **Consumer safeguards are currently inadequate to protect against online advertising abuses, including malware, invasive cookies, and inappropriate data collection.** Cybercriminals are constantly finding new ways to evade existing security methods. Self-regulatory codes do not significantly address online advertising security, and data collection protections are often limited in scope, and underutilized. Current FTC safeguards are insufficient to comprehensively protect consumers from online advertising abuses.

6. **Current systems may not create sufficient incentives for online advertising participants to prevent consumer abuses.** Because responsibility for malware attacks and inappropriate data collection through online advertisements is undefined, online advertising participants may not be fully incentivized to establish effective consumer safeguards against abuses.

Recommendations

Based upon the Subcommittee's investigation, the Report makes the following recommendations.

1. **Establish better practices and clearer rules to prevent online advertising abuses.** Under the current regulatory and legislative framework, legal responsibility for damages caused through malvertising usually rests only with the fraudulent actor in question. Since such actors are rarely caught and even less frequently able to pay damages, the harm caused by malicious advertisements is ultimately born by consumers who in many cases have done nothing more than visit a mainstream website. While consumers should be careful to keep their operating systems and programs updated to avoid vulnerability, sophisticated commercial entities, large and small, should take steps to reduce systemic vulnerabilities in their advertising networks. If sophisticated commercial entities do not take steps to further protect consumers, regulatory or legislative change may be needed so that such entities are incentivized to increase security for advertisements run through their systems.

2. **Strengthen security information exchanges within the online advertising industry to prevent abuses.** Some online advertising companies claim they do not share information about security hazards with other companies, because of fears they will be accused of violating antitrust laws by cooperating with competitors. The

Department of Justice and the Federal Trade Commission recently issued joint guidance suggesting that the sharing of cyber threat-related information would not trigger antitrust liability. Those agencies should clarify the extent to which online advertising participants may exchange information about security hazards without incurring antitrust or other liability. If necessary, Congress should pass legislation that removes legal impediments to the sharing of actionable cyber-threat related information and creates incentives for the voluntary sharing of information.

3. **Clarify specific prohibited practices in online advertising to prevent abuses and protect consumers.** Self-regulatory bodies should endeavor to develop comprehensive security guidelines for preventing online advertising malware attacks. In the absence of effective self-regulation, the FTC should consider issuing comprehensive regulations to prohibit deceptive and unfair online advertising practices that facilitate or fail to take reasonable steps to prevent malware, invasive cookies, and inappropriate data collection delivered to Internet consumers through online advertisements. Greater specificity in prohibited or discouraged practices is needed before the overall security situation in the online advertising industry can improve.

4. **Develop additional "circuit breakers" to protect consumers.** Given the complexity of the online advertising ecosystem, more "circuit breakers" should be incorporated into the online advertising system, systems that introduce check-points that ensure malicious advertisements are caught at an earlier stage before transmission to consumers. Online advertising industry participants should thoroughly vet new advertisers and perform rigorous and ongoing checks as often as feasible to ensure that advertisements that appear legitimate upon initial submission remain so.

II. BACKGROUND

In order to understand some of the hazards consumers face in the online advertising industry, it is necessary to understand two different processes: (1) how data is collected on Internet users by third parties and (2) how online advertisements are delivered while making use of that data. The online advertising industry has evolved to make extensive use of those two processes, presenting challenges to consumer safety and privacy today.

a. Data Collection in the Online Advertising Industry

1. Cookies

Since the inception of the Internet, cookies have been the primary tools by which companies transmit information about Internet users.[24] Best conceptualized as an identity card for a particular machine that accesses the Internet, cookies are small text files placed on an Internet user's computer hard drive or browser that store information about a user's interactions with a particular website.[25] When an Internet user visits a website, the user's browser sends a request to the website's server to load the page in question. In addition to the request for the page, the user's browser is programmed to send along information from any cookies placed by the website's server. If there are no such cookies—either because the user has never visited the website before or because she has deleted the cookies on her hard drive—the website's server may assign a new cookie for use in the current session and potentially on subsequent visits.

The most basic function a cookie serves is to identify a device. With a cookie, websites can know how many unique machines—and, by extension, roughly how many unique visitors— come to their site. By allowing a website to identify individual visitors, cookies can help websites provide useful services to visitors. For example, many anti-fraud provisions are cookie-based, and most online "shopping cart" functions need a cookie to confirm that the user who added one item to their cart is the same user who has navigated to a different part of the website.

2. First-Party vs. Third-Party Cookies

A cookie that is placed by the website a user actually visits is called a first-party cookie. If a user visits an online shopping website, she might have a cookie placed on her machine so that the company can recognize the user when she move to another page on the site and remember what she put into her online shopping cart.

By contrast, a third-party cookie is one placed by a website other than the one the user directly accessed. If a user visits most ordinary websites (e.g., a newspaper website or a blog), some third party (or third parties) will likely place a cookie on that user's computer. Almost every website examined by the

Subcommittee called some third party or parties who operated cookies on that website.[26] As discussed above, a cookie is placed in response to a browser's request to load a page. When a user visits a website that runs a third-party cookie, the host website instructs the user's browser to contact the third-party. The third party sends back whatever content the user's browser requested, as well as a cookie. This interaction can be displayed schematically as follows.

3. Tracking Users Through Cookies

While cookies themselves simply identify machines, Internet companies can use cookies as a proxy for a single user's online activities. An ad network's cookie might note, to use a fictitious example, that one unique user first visited "www.FreshCooking.com", then "www.FreshCooking.com/vegan." The ad network can read the webpage uniform resource locators (URLs) and, of course, access the content on FreshCooking.com itself and infer that the user in question is interested in cooking.[27] It can cross-reference that information with any other recent website visits by that user that it detected through its cookie network (say, a visit to "www.MeatFree.com").[28] Knowing even only some of the user's browsing history can allow an ad network to conclude with a high degree of certainty that the user in question is a vegetarian. It can then use that information to deliver targeted advertisements to that user.

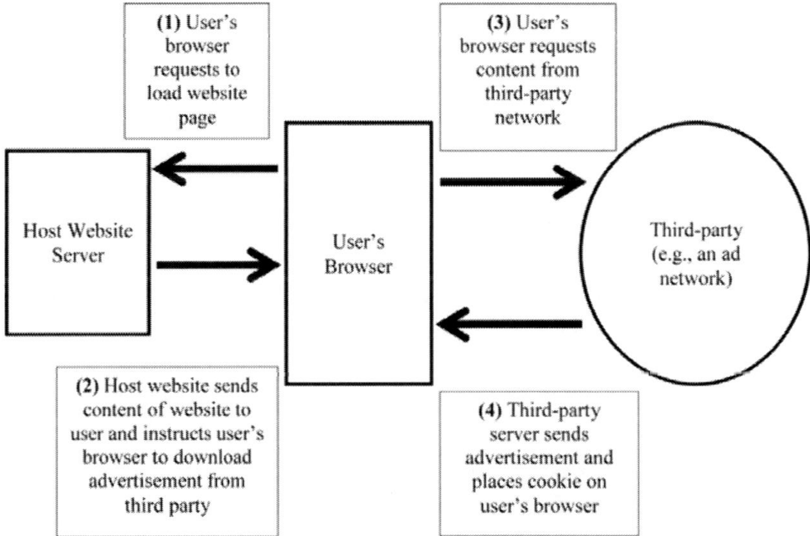

Figure 1. Third-party cookie placement on a user's machine.

4. Data Collection and Advertising

Ad networks are the most prominent third-party cookie users because (a) they directly benefit from the collection of user information and (b) they have a built-in opportunity to deliver cookies every time they deliver an ad. As discussed in a later section in the report, ad networks use the data they collect from cookies to target advertisements as precisely as possible to particular users, trying to infer as much information as they can about each user's location, interests, and demographic information. The more data these ad networks can collect from different websites on a particular user, the better the inferences they can draw.

The built-in opportunity to deliver a cookie stems from the fact that the host website's server has to contact the ad network every time it needs an ad. While the ad network does not deliver the advertisement itself—a distinction which will become vitally important in the context of malware—the host website's server's call to the ad network allows the ad network to place a cookie.

Ad networks are not the only companies that operate cookies across multiple websites. Data brokers like Acxiom and BlueKai, who collect information on consumers in order to facilitate the targeting of advertisements, have also contracted to place and access their cookies across multiple websites. As discussed above, third parties can deliver a cookie because some part of the host website draws upon content from the third-party server. In the context of advertising, the third-party content requested by the host website is the advertisement itself. A call from the host website opens the door for a cookie to be placed by the third party whose content was called for. However, the third-party content displayed on the host website can be almost invisible— it is very often a single pixel on the screen.[29] Because the host website requested some nominal amount of content from the third-party—even if the content is just a single pixel—the third-party can now deliver its cookie to the user's browser as well. Thus, data brokers or other entities that deliver no real content to the host website can still deliver cookies by contracting with the host website to place a single pixel on their website.[30]

5. Cookie Controversies

The ability to place cookies is highly valuable to ad networks. In fact, advertisers are willing to pay a premium of between 60 and 200 percent for targeted advertisements based on cookies.[31] The privacy implications are equally clear. Cookies can in theory be used to infer damaging personal information about particular users, such as the fact that a user has a certain medical condition. Even less immediately controversial inferences, like the age of a user, can enable criminals to target the very young or elderly with fraudulent advertisements.

Generally, a browser's default settings leave cookies active, since many benign web functions consumers have come to expect are cookie based. A privacy minded (and tech-savvy) user can avoid all cookie-based tracking if she so chooses. However, very few Internet users actually alter default browser settings that prioritize consumer privacy.[32] The default browser setting therefore makes a tremendous difference in the use of cookies, and consequently how much data is gathered on Internet users.

Furthermore, despite some interest by browser developers to block certain types of cookies, this does not always lead to better consumer privacy. For example, when Apple announced that its Safari browser's default setting would block third-party cookies, Google used a "workaround" that enabled it to place cookies despite the default setting. Google ultimately agreed to pay a $22.5 million fine to the FTC for that "deceptive" practice.[33] Mozilla also announced that it would block third-party cookies by default in its Firefox browser, but actual implementation has been delayed several times and the online advertising industry has voiced strong disapproval of the measure.[34]

b. How Online Advertisements Are Delivered

1. Simplified Process of Ad Delivery

Online advertisements may appear to be part of the host website that a user visits, just like images in an article online, but they are different in several important respects. First, and most crucially, the advertisements delivered through ad networks are generally not under the control of the host website at the time of delivery. The ads usually do not physically reside on the same server as the main content of the website. Second, while an advertisement in a newspaper is just a static picture, online advertisements can deliver files and whole programs to a user even if the advertisement itself appears to be just an image.

When a user visits a website that uses an ad network to deliver its ads, the host website instructs the user's browser to contact the ad network. The ad network, in turn, retrieves whatever user cookie identifiers it can. Using those identifiers, the ad network can access its own database to see what other information about the user's history it has in order to identify the user's interests and demographic information. The ad network can then decide which advertisement would be best to serve that particular user.

Though the ad network decides which advertisement should be sent, it often does not deliver the actual advertisements. Instead, the ad network instructs the user's browser to contact a server designated by the actual advertiser. The server that delivers the advertisement is most often called a content delivery network (CDN). It is most often a separate, stand-alone entity, and thus represents another potential vulnerability within the advertising delivery process.

The advertiser's designated server then delivers the actual image or video to the user's browser. All of those steps cumulatively occur over the course of about one second.

Two caveats must be made about this summary. First, the actual delivery process can end up being far more complicated. The ad network can go through any number of exchanges and other online advertising companies which exist to help ad networks target a user as precisely as possible. Several experts told the Subcommittee that the actual number of intermediary companies between the host website and the advertiser averages around 5 or 6 in many cases. Those other online advertising companies are discussed at length in another section. For purposes of this section of the report, it is sufficient to note that the ad network (or other companies) that chooses which advertisement to deliver does not control the actual delivery of that ad, which is a source of a great deal of security vulnerability in the industry. Second, this depiction obviously applies only to typical third-party delivered advertisements, not direct sales or other variations that might be found within the online advertising industry.

2. The Role of Ad Tags in the Online Ad Delivery Process

Another important aspect of ad delivery is the complicated manner in which the user's browser, the host website, the ad network, and the advertiser communicate with each other. That communication is ultimately achieved through "ad tags," which are hypertext markup language (HTML) code sent between online advertising entities, which will ultimately call up the correct advertisement to be delivered to a user.[35] That HTML code conveys information about the advertisement space to be filled. The ad tag includes basic details about the size of the space to be filled as well as cookie-based identifiers to facilitate targeting of the ad. The functioning of ad tags explains how online advertising companies can send advertisements to users' browsers without the advertising companies actually directly knowing what that advertisement is.

Ad tags are the messages that tell online advertising companies what ad to deliver without actually having to send the advertisement itself between multiple companies. When a user visits a website, that host website sends an ad tag out to its ad network. That tag will contain some form of cookie identification so that the ad network will recognize the user. The host website does not need to know anything about the user in order to facilitate data collection; all it must do is notify the ad network of the user's cookie identifier.[36] The ad network's server will then rapidly call up all available data on the user and decide which advertisement to deliver (or call upon another outside party to decide which advertisement to deliver). The ad network will then send an ad tag back through the user's browser, telling it to retrieve the proper advertisement at a URL that the advertiser (the customer of the ad network) has specified.

This is where a key vulnerability in the online advertising system lies. The ad network often performs some manner of initial quality control on the advertisement by examining what happens when it calls the particular URL of the advertiser. However, the actual file at that URL can be quietly changed after that initial quality control check so that when a user actually encounters the ad, an innocuous and safe ad may have been transformed into a vehicle for malware.[37]

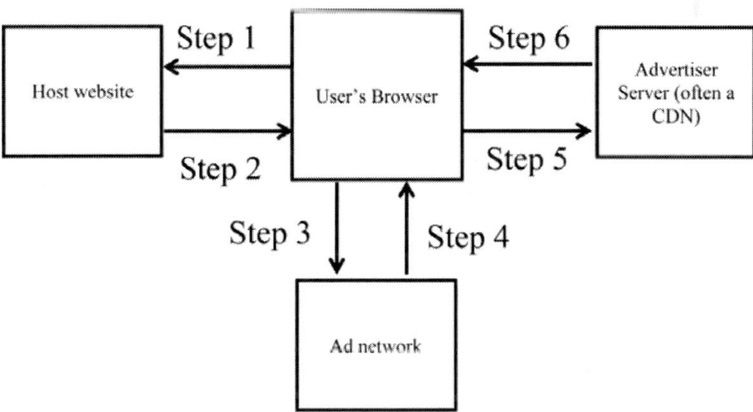

Figure 2. A simplified depiction of the ad delivery process.

3. Direct Sale Advertisements vs. Ad Network Advertisements

Not all online advertisements are delivered through ad networks. Some websites still sell many of their own advertisements directly. Most "floating" ads, where an advertisement obscures the content of a website, are sold directly.[38] Because such advertisements are highly intrusive, websites are reluctant to entrust ad networks to choose advertisements that could reflect poorly on the website.

Most direct sales of advertisements are made by popular websites to large advertisers whose products are directly complementary to the website's focus. Because of the complementary nature of the product and the website, there is less need for targeting ads in the way an ad network can. For example, CNN, a news site, can directly sell advertisements to HBO for its parody news program "Last Week Tonight" and coordinate banner, sidebar, and interactive components of the same advertisement.[39]

While direct sales minimize user data transmission because they are often untargeted, they also remove the quality-control processes available to ad networks. The host websites are sometimes less technologically sophisticated than ad networks, which can lead to additional vulnerabilities, as will be discussed at length in Part III of this report.

Figure 3. Example of direct-sale advertisement, where CNN coordinated the sale of multiple ad- spaces to HBO. Note the ads for "Last Week Tonight" on the left, right, top, and middle of CNN's front page.

Figure 4. Depiction of an advertiser directly buying ad space from a publisher.

c. Evolution of the Online Advertising Industry

The online advertising ecosystem has significantly evolved over the years to reflect the intricate expansion of the Internet. Today, the online advertising ecosystem is more than just an exchange of advertisements and money – it is an exchange of information that continues to grow as more users access the Internet and either knowingly or unknowingly share their personal data with an attentive and vibrant online advertising market.

Originally, advertisements were exchanged online between an advertiser (or an ad agency) and a publisher (a website). The advertiser directly bought ad space or inventory from a publisher and then transmitted its advertisement to the publisher's website(s) for public display, much like a billboard near a highway. Each time a particular advertisement was displayed, it was called a single impression.[40]

1. The Rise of Ad Networks

As publishers created more websites and the opportunity for online advertising increased, advertisers wanted to expand their presence on the Internet and buy more ad space, or "inventory" for specific audiences (based on age, gender, interests, location, etc.). However, it was difficult for advertisers to reach target audience members because, according to online industry experts, Internet audiences were "incredibly fragmented, splitting their online time between many different websites."[41] Advertisers needed a neutral party to analyze the increasing amount of advertising space from publishers to be able to transmit their advertisements to the right users despite audience fragmentation.[42] At the same time, publishers needed a way to efficiently sell their inventory and fill in their ad spaces.[43]

Thus, in 1997, ad networks were established to serve as a conduit between the advertisers and the publishers.[44] Originally, ad networks would receive inventory from publishers like sports magazines or news websites and aggregate or "package" this data into different categories based on age, gender, interests, etc.[45] Ad networks would sell these "packages" to advertisers based on the type of audience the advertiser was targeting.

For example, in the figure below a shoe company and its ad agency may want to run a campaign targeted at male sports fans ages 18 to 24. The shoe company would send this request to an ad network. The ad network, which contracts with publishers, has acquired and packaged ad space, or "inventory", and offers to sell the shoe company inventory packages. The shoe company reviews these packages and buys inventory that best matches its ad campaign's audience segment. Based on the type of inventory package the shoe company purchased, the ad network then transmits the shoe company's advertisement to the publisher providing the selected inventory – a newspaper website in this example.

2. The Weaknesses of Ad Networks

While the ad networks provided advertisers an opportunity to target specific audience segments, the process in which the ad networks bought, packaged, and sold inventory created challenges for advertisers and publishers alike.[46] Ad networks often offered advertisers little insight into where advertisements were ultimately placed.[47] This resulted in advertisers often having to buy inventory "blindly" and then wait, sometimes for several months, to see whether their ad campaign was effective.[48]

Additionally, ad networks did not place value on specific ad space and only provided advertisers a set price for an inventory package that contained millions of ad spaces.[49] This resulted in advertisers purchasing ad spaces in bulk that might not necessarily attract viewers that are the best match for their ad campaign.[50] Thus, advertisers were essentially spending money on a package of ad spaces that were only partially on target.[51]

Furthermore, in some cases advertisers would buy inventory packages from an ad network that might not collect or sell inventory data from a publisher that would be the best match for the advertiser's targeted audience. In the example above, the shoe company's preferred target audience frequently visits the sports news website. However, the shoe company's ad network may not collect or sell inventory data from the sports news website, which could deal solely with a different ad network. Thus, even though the shoe company's advertisements are ultimately displayed online to some members of its target audience who visit the newspaper website, the shoe company would be unable to reach members of its target audience who access the sports news website.

In order to avoid this challenge, advertisers would contract with multiple ad networks in an attempt to ensure that their advertisements would eventually reach as many targeted audience segments as possible. However, this method also proved problematic since advertisers were now blindly buying inventory packages from multiple ad networks without insight into where their advertisements were displayed. In some cases, advertisers were buying the same audience segment more than once.[52]

Publishers also faced great difficulties with the ad network process. Ad networks did not offer publishers a way to identify the best advertisers for their websites. Additionally, publishers would usually work with a series of ad networks in case one would fail to sell its inventory.[53] This resulted in many different parties taking a cut from the publisher's ad space revenue.[54]

Use of the ad networks was meant to simplify the exchange of information between and among advertisers and publishers by aggregating data into unique inventory packages. However, due to the ad networks' lack of transparency and their imprecise valuations of ad space, the online advertising industry desperately needed a new business model to promote and efficiently advance the exchange of data in a way that was beneficial to both advertisers and publishers.[55]

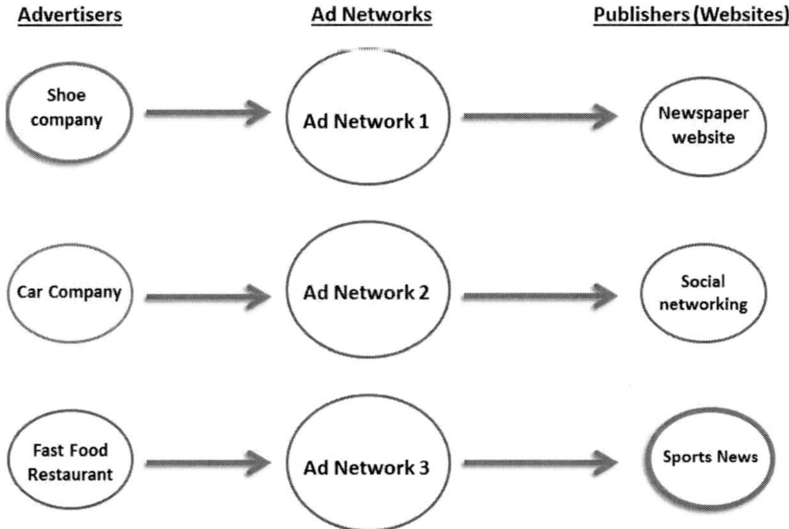

Figure 5. Depiction of online advertising process through ad networks.

3. A New Business Model: The Ad Exchanges

In 2005 the online advertising industry saw the birth of the ad exchanges—a new online advertising business model that would solve many of the problems created by the ad networks.[56] Whereas the ad networks forced advertisers into buying ad spaces in bulk (via inventory packages), the ad exchanges offered advertisers the chance to buy ad space individually.[57] On an ad-by-ad basis, advertisers could choose where they wanted their advertisement to be displayed and how much they were willing to pay for a particular ad space.

As shown in the figure below, when a person visits a publisher's website (Step One), that publisher will send out a request to an ad exchange to fill the website's ad space with advertisements that will be displayed to that particular user (Step Two).[58] In its request to the ad exchange, the publisher will provide the user's unique cookie identifier and information on the type of ad space available (e.g., ad space size).[59] Next, the ad exchange passes along the publisher's advertisement criteria as well as information the exchange has collected on the user to participating advertisers in the exchange (Step Three).[60] At this time, advertisers bid against one another in real time for this particular ad space to be displayed to this particular user (Step Four).[61] This process is called "real-time bidding."[62] To give a sense of the scale of online advertising, the typical cost for a thousand ad impressions (views of an individual ad) ranges from about $0.50 to $17 depending on the subject of the advertisement and the quality of the host website.[63] The ad exchange will then select the highest bidder (Step Five) and send that advertisement to the publisher's website (Step Six) where the ad space is filled with the ad image (Step Seven) and finally displayed to the user (Step Eight).[64] This entire process usually takes less than a second.[65]

The ad exchanges offer valuable information to publishers and advertisers alike. On the advertising side, the ad exchange can offer advertisers insight into what ads are performing well and where those ads are being displayed so advertisers can adjust their campaigns to maximize the impact of their ads.[66] On the publishing side, the ad exchange can provide valuable information to publishers on what advertiser or ad agency is buying that publisher's inventory and how much they are paying for it.[67] This level of insight offered by the ad exchanges is a major improvement from former ad network models.[68]

Additionally, since advertisers buy impressions (views of an ad) individually as opposed to "packaged" deals (as offered by ad networks), they are able to buy specific ad space at much higher prices since they can buy only the impressions they specifically want.[69] As a result of advertisers only buying impressions that they deem valuable, the level of competition for each ad space drives up the price for each impression on a website, with advertisers willing to pay a premium of between 60 and 200 percent,[70] which ultimately results in more revenue for the publishers, compared to the noncompetitive environment of the ad network model.[71]

4. The Weakness of Ad Exchanges

While ad exchanges offer many improvements to ad network structures, both are still similar in the sense that advertisers can only bid on ad space from a finite amount of publishers that contract with a particular ad exchange. Thus, since advertisers are limited in the amount of publishers they can reach, they are equally limited in the amount of users they can access as well. Essentially, the ad exchange model alone still leaves advertisers requiring a way to be able to reach across the entire online advertising industry and participate in real-time bidding on ad space from publishers in and outside their ad exchange.

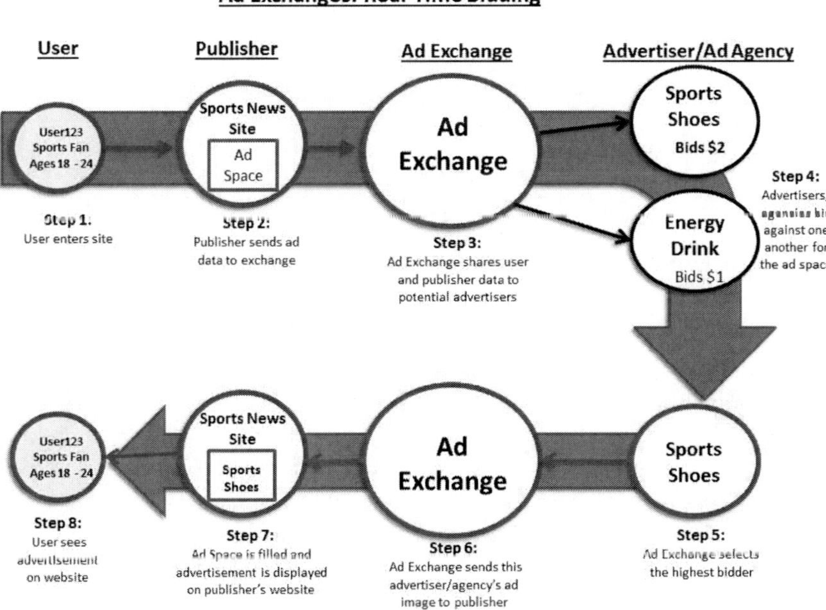

Figure 6. Depiction of the online advertising process with ad exchanges.

5. Reaching across the Online Advertising Industry: Demand-Side Platforms

Demand-side platforms (DSPs) are companies that allow advertisers to extend their "virtual" reach across the online advertising ecosystem. Instead of participating with a single ad exchange, advertisers contract with a DSP, which then enters multiple ad exchanges on behalf of the advertiser. This allows advertisers more access to users who view websites owned by different publishers that contract with different ad exchanges.

In the example below, the shoe company might have an advertisement targeted toward sports fans aged 18-24. The shoe company would send this information to a DSP, which then scans the ad exchanges for bids on websites viewed by sports fans aged 18-24. The DSP may find two ad exchanges that are currently auctioning ad space on the sports news website and a sporting goods store's website respectively, which have just been accessed by members of the shoe company's target audience. The DSP enters a bidding process on behalf of the shoe company and wins the ad space in both ad exchanges. The shoe company's advertisement is then transmitted and displayed to the particular users on the sports news website and the sporting goods store's website, which both meet the shoe company's target audience criteria. Supply-side platforms work in the same manner, but on the publisher side instead of the advertiser side. They enter multiple exchanges for publishers in order to find the highest-bid advertiser.

d. The Role of Self-Regulatory Groups

Although the FTC can and does bring enforcement actions against individual companies, self-regulatory groups currently generate the most specific standards for the behavior of companies in the online advertising industry. Many online advertising companies adhere to standards generated by the Digital Advertising Alliance (DAA) and Network Advertising Initiative (NAI) that govern behavioral advertising and data collection.

Each of those organizations has put forward a code with general guidelines for companies that engage in online advertising. These codes are predominately written and approved by major industry players, with varying, but limited, levels of consumer input.[72] Those organizations do not deal in large part with security issues pertaining to malware in online advertising.

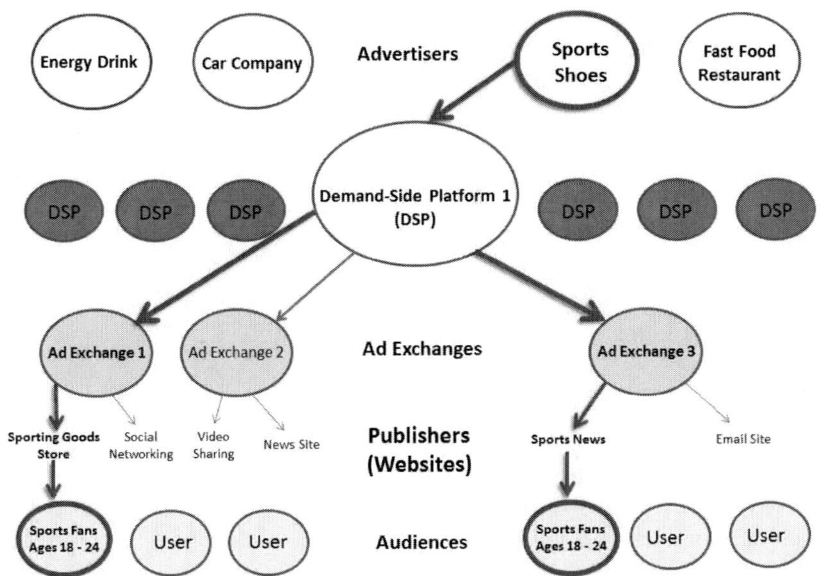

Figure 7. Online advertising process with a demand-side platform.

e. Data Brokers

The FTC has defined "data brokers" as "companies that collect information, including personal information about consumers, from a wide variety of sources for the purpose of reselling such information to their customers for various purposes, including verifying an individual's identity, differentiating records, marketing products, and preventing financial fraud."[73] In the context of the online advertising industry, the information that data brokers collect and then resell to online businesses (advertisers, ad networks, ad exchanges, publishers, etc.) can help those companies compile data on particular users and then better target online advertisements to those individuals. Yet, many concerns have been raised about the lack of transparency regarding the practices of data brokers, specifically the data brokers' ability to collect a wealth of information on consumers without the consumer ever knowing that this collection is taking place.[74]

In December 2013, the U.S. Senate Committee on Commerce, Science, and Transportation released a Majority Staff Report that focused on the data broker industry and highlighted data broker activities regarding the collection, use, and sale of consumer data for marketing purposes.[75] The staff report found that data brokers collect a vast amount of detailed information on millions of consumers including data points on people's financial status, what type of car they drive, what types of pets they have, and even whether the consumer is suffering from a medical condition.[76] Additionally, the staff report found that many data brokers, without any consumer permission or knowledge, create profiles of consumers that are financially vulnerable and sell that information to other businesses that are targeting individuals in need of quick cash, loans, or other financial products.[77]

The report found that data brokers combine information on consumers collected both online and "offline" in order to compile the most complete set of data points about a particular person. Essentially, in addition to collecting consumer information online from sources on the Internet, data brokers also store and sell information on consumers concerning their activities offline including purchases and interests.[78] There is little a consumer can do to "opt-out" of their offline activities. Moreover, given the "veil of secrecy" behind which data brokers operate, it is unclear the extent to which consumers can limit data brokers' access to their personal information that is compiled and eventually sold without consumer consent or knowledge.[79]

III. ONLINE ADVERTISING AND HIDDEN HAZARDS TO CONSUMER SECURITY AND DATA PRIVACY

Through its investigation, the Subcommittee identified a number of hidden hazards to consumers in the online advertising industry. Prominent among these hazards is malicious software ("malware") delivered through online advertising without any clicks or interaction by a user. Furthermore, the data collection that makes online advertising possible also allows cybercriminals to target their activities against vulnerable users. As the online advertising industry becomes more and more complex and fragmented, there may be less accountability for individual participants. Although the companies themselves also suffer reputational or other damage from these attacks, consumers are often left with little, if any, meaningful remedy for their damages. Self-regulatory bodies could provide stronger oversight to ensure safety in the online advertising arena from these sorts of hazards.

a. Case Studies: Emerging Dangers in Online Advertising

The Subcommittee's investigation revealed a number of dangers to online users which have already caused significant damage to consumers. For each vulnerability, Subcommittee staff identified actual cases where the vulnerability has already been exploited.

1. Malware from Online Advertising Can Do Damage without Clicks: YouTube/Google Ad Attack, February 2014

Two of the most important facts discovered by the Subcommittee in its investigation are (1) that malware in online advertising often does not require any clicking on ads by the user, and (2) malware delivered through advertising is found on the most reputable, most popular sites on the Internet and can be delivered through the biggest, most technologically sophisticated ad networks. One incident that highlights both points was a malware attack through Google's ad network that was delivered to users on YouTube.[80]

In February 2014, a security engineer discovered that a YouTube link was hosting malware. When she followed up on the lead, she discovered that the malware was actually delivered via an advertisement.[81] A user did not actually need to click on any ads on YouTube; just watching a video was enough to lead to an infection.[82] The malware in question would examine a consumer's computer and, when it found whatever machines fit its criteria, it would release a "banking Trojan" virus—designed to break into online bank accounts and transfer funds to a cybercriminal's account.[83] That malware was designed to target users with unpatched versions of Internet Explorer. Google worked with the security engineer to identify the exact ads in question and took steps to prevent a recurrence of similar attacks.[84]

An unwitting consumer who visited YouTube and encountered this malware would have no opportunity to protect herself from potential financial ruin. If she suffered an attack, she would have little recourse unless she managed to track down the cybercriminal who launched the attack, an almost impossible task for security professionals and completely beyond the capabilities of an ordinary consumer.

2. The Complexity of the Online Advertising Industry Leads to Multiple Points of Vulnerability: Major League Baseball's Website Delivers Malware, June 2012

The vision of the online advertising industry as companies that simply connect website publishers and advertisers does not reflect the multiple layers of complexity that have been added over the past decade. A routine advertisement often goes through five or six intermediaries before ending upon a user's browser. The advertiser will often work through a separate advertising agency, marketer, ad exchange, demand-side platform, *and* ad network before an ad actually reaches the user's browser. Each time one of those entities passes along a call for an advertisement, there is an opportunity for the introduction of malware. With more opportunities for bad software to enter the system, each participant has a better case to make that it is not responsible for system-wide security, and it becomes that much more difficult to determine where along the chain something went wrong.

One incident where this point was made clear was the website of Major League Baseball (MLB) in June 2012.[85] Many visitors to MLB's popular website MLB.com were exposed to a malicious advertisement that, when clicked on, downloaded a virus to the user's computer.[86] This malicious ad, which had the potential to impact 300,000 users, was delivered to MLB.com through a compromised ad network that began distributing malware.[87] The ad in question was an advertisement for luxury watches that was displayed as a banner at the top of the MLB webpage.

According to reports, when users clicked on the ad, they were prompted to download fake anti-virus software that "pretends to scan the victim's computer, find files it claims are infected, and then attempts to get the victim to purchase the 'Full Version' to remove the non-existent threats for the low, low price of $99.99."[89]

This malware attack only came to light after it was discovered by an online security company, Perimeter's Security Operations Center. Researchers from that company suspected that this attack was a result of an infected ad network that distributed the malicious ad to MLB.com. Evan Keiser, a security analyst at Perimeter described vulnerabilities in the online advertising industry that resulted in the MLB malvertising attack:

> "Sadly, this has become an extremely common issue: well-known and respected websites inadvertently distribute malware due to one of their hosted syndicated ads being compromised... The website operator provides a spot [...] where an ad network loads its ads. Many of these ad networks, in turn, load content from syndication partners and from other ad networks. At some point down the chain, one of these partners source the web ad from the advertiser's web server. Because of the multiple layers of syndication between the website and originating ad server, it can be often very hard to understand exactly where the ad actually originated.

It's only a slight exaggeration to say that the lack of transparency and multiple indirect relationships can be so complicated that the average ad network makes the Fulton Fish Market look like the New York Stock Exchange by comparison."[90]

The fact that the source of an attack can remain a mystery even after detection further highlights the lack of accountability within the online advertising industry. Incentives to provide security are weakened by the fact that many malware attacks are either never discovered or never publicly attributed to a particular ad network or other online advertising entity.

3. Online Advertising Malware Attack Coordinated to Hit at Vulnerable Times: Yahoo Malware Attack, December 2013-January 2014

As anyone who works in an office can attest, Friday afternoons can sometimes bring a lull in activity. Federal holidays are another time when office staffing is minimized. Cybercriminals who exploit the online advertising industry are aware of those facts as well. They deliberately coordinate their attacks to commence at a time when they believe there are as few quality-control personnel at the various advertising companies as possible. Law enforcement personnel have even discovered calendars at the office and residences of cybercriminals in Russia with all federal holidays carefully marked and noted.[91]

Figure 8. A screenshot of MLB.com which shows the malicious ad at the top of the webpage.[88]

On Friday, December 27, 2013—two days after Christmas and four days before New Year's Eve—cybercriminals began injecting malware-ridden advertisements into Yahoo's ad network. While Yahoo had security personnel working through the holidays, the cybercriminals in question were nevertheless successful in their attack. The malware-infected advertisements continued to run until January 3, 2014, when Yahoo discovered the problem, took the ads off their network, and initiated tighter security protocols to prevent future attacks.[92] Though Yahoo initially reported that the advertisements were delivered only to Internet users in Europe,[93] later reports suggest that machines outside of the European Union were also compromised.[94]

The malware in question spread without the need for user interaction. Users did not need to click on suspicious-looking ads.[95] Indeed, the advertisement in question was not even visible to the victims who visited ordinary websites. Instead, when a user visited a website with Yahoo ads delivered, the user's browser, at Yahoo's direction, contacted the advertiser's server, which delivered malware to the user's browser instead of the image of an advertisement. The malware then seized control of the user's computer and used it to generate Bitcoins, a digital currency that requires a tremendous amount of computer power to actually create.[96]

In this case, the advertisement made it past Yahoo's security protocols because a hacker had gained access to a Yahoo employee's account and approved the malicious advertisement in question.[97] The attack utilized Yahoo's ad network as a delivery system, but gained access to that system through the sort of hacking that has been going on for years.

Independent security firms estimate that around 27,000 computers were infected through this one malware-laden advertisement.[98] Around 300,000 visitors were exposed to the advertisement, yielding an infection rate of around 9 percent.[99] The virus in question would not trigger on any random computer, but only ones with particular operating systems and programs,[100] making the virus even more difficult to detect through the ordinary scanning implemented by ad networks and security firms and discussed in detail in the next section.[101]

That vulnerability within the network emerged simply because a single Yahoo employee's account was compromised. The Subcommittee's investigation indicates that other ad networks may also be vulnerable to that method of attack. Yahoo, it appears, meets industry standard practice for security in its advertisements. However, the industry standard appears to fall short of the level required to comprehensively protect consumers who visit popular websites from malvertising.

4. Ad Networks Do Not Directly Deliver the Advertisements They Place, Limiting the Effectiveness of Their Security Measures: "JS:Prontexi" Malware Attack on Multiple Ad Networks, 2010

As discussed in the Background section, ad networks do not deliver the actual image or substantive advertisement (referred to in the online advertising industry as the "creative") that appears on a consumer's browser. Because the ad network must engage in millions of these information exchanges each second, it needs a tremendous amount of bandwidth even to simply retrieve small cookie text files. If the ad network were to host the images for each advertisement itself, its bandwidth needs could be thousands of times greater because image files are so much larger than simple text files. To save on bandwidth and decrease the amount of time it takes to load webpages, the images for the advertisements are kept on another server, which is many times owned by an entity separate from the advertiser.

Because ad networks do not deliver the advertisements they place, they need to perform quality control on the advertisements through two basic processes: human oversight and automated scanning. Ad networks regularly deliver millions of ads per minute, a computationally intensive process requiring powerful networked servers. Ads must be selected and delivered in well-under a second, and consequently there is pressure to deliver ads quickly and not tie up server resources and time doing quality control.

Scanning is the automated process in place for quality-control purposes and is actually a reasonably simple concept. The scanning process replicates a situation in which machines located at a few locations around the world load webpages where advertisements run and monitor what they actually do when running on a user browser. When the advertisements are run through scanning processes, they are tested against multiple browser types, decomposed into component parts, and tested for known viruses or calls to known malicious URLs.[102]

Cybercriminals routinely attempt to circumvent scanning with several inventive tactics. First, just like ordinary advertisers, cybercriminals can target their malware to execute on only certain devices in specific geographic locations.[103] In the most basic sense, if the cybercriminals know that the scanners are located in, for example, Palo Alto and New York City, they might direct their malware-laden advertisements to run only in Ames, Iowa. Second, cybercriminals are becoming increasingly adept targeting the types of machines and operating systems their ads run on. With a plethora of machines and operating systems to choose from, it is almost impossible for scanners to test every device and every configuration.

Those deficiencies help explain how one particular malware attack, the "JS:Prontexi" virus, avoided detection by many major online advertising companies in 2010.[104] The spread of that malware was one of the first published accounts where an advertising malware threat occurred with no user interaction or clicks. JS:Prontexi targeted only Windows operating system users and specialized further by focusing on vulnerabilities in Adobe Reader, Adobe Acrobat, Flash, Java, and QuickTime.[105] Over the course of four months, the JS:Prontexi virus spread to 2.6 million computers.[106] 16,300 of those instances of the virus were delivered through Google's subsidiary DoubleClick, and another 530,000 were from a Yahoo-controlled ad network.[107] The JS:Prontexi virus spread for over four months before its existence was disclosed to the public by a security company.[108]

Both Yahoo and Google claimed at the time to have detected the malicious advertisement, but apparently only after many users' computers were infected with the JS:Prontexi virus.[109] The difficulty that even the most sophisticated ad networks face in providing comprehensive security suggests that the countless other entities that comprise the online advertising industry may also struggle to maintain security at their companies.

5. *Epic Marketplace and the Limitations of Self-Regulatory Bodies, 2010-2011*

The online advertising industry's self-regulatory groups are tasked with maintaining industry standards for privacy and security. The theory of self-regulation is that membership in such a regulatory body is an indication to consumers of quality and trustworthiness. Many online advertisers hold up their membership in such organizations as evidence of the propriety of their operations.[110] The Subcommittee's investigation has found few instances of companies being expelled or suspended from one of these organizations for non-compliance with the organization's code. Even after wrongdoing is discovered by entities other than the regulators, offending companies are sometimes not suspended or excluded from membership in any of those organizations.

For example, in March 2010, Epic Marketplace, an online advertising company, began to engage in "history sniffing," a method by which a company can determine whether a consumer has previously visited a webpage by examining how the user's browser displays hyperlinks (purple indicating visited hyperlinks, blue indicating non-visited hyperlinks.)[111] History sniffing can be an even more powerful tool for data collection than cookies—it enables companies to record user visits to websites outside of its cookie network.

Through this practice, Epic Marketplace could see that users had visited pages relating to, among other things, fertility issues, impotence, menopause, incontinence, disability insurance, credit repair, debt relief, and personal bankruptcy.[112] Based on that knowledge, Epic Marketplace could identify user interest segments in those areas and use the information for targeted advertisements.[113]

The practice was discovered by Stanford Security Lab in July 2011. Epic Marketplace's privacy policy had stated that "[w]eb surfers may elect not to provide non-personally identifiable information by following the cookie opt-out procedures set forth [on its website]."[114] Because Epic Marketplace's history sniffing contradicted its privacy policy, the FTC brought an enforcement action against Epic Marketplace. The FTC approved a final order settling charges against Epic Marketplace in March 2013.[115]

Epic Marketplace was a member of NAI at the time the practice came to light. Despite that fact, NAI's audits did not discover Epic Marketplace's history sniffing practice. Once Epic Marketplace's misbehavior came to light, NAI said that it would launch its own investigation.[116] During that time, Epic Marketplace remained an NAI member, subjected merely to additional auditing requirements.[117] Subsequently, Epic Marketplace went out of business, removing it from NAI's membership lists.

To the extent that the self-regulatory codes are binding, actual detection and punishment of noncompliance is remarkably rare. NAI recently completed its 2013 Compliance Report and, after reviewing 88 members, "NAI still did not find any material noncompliance with [its] Code."[118]

6. Direct Sales of Advertisements Are Subject to Compromise: New York Times Malware Attack, 2009

Some major websites sell their advertising through direct sales to advertisers, bypassing most of the technology companies who have traditionally dominated the online advertising industry. Direct sales can, in some ways, be beneficial for security: with fewer parties involved, there are fewer ways in which criminals can slip in malware. As one security researcher noted: "I think there is a problem with ad networks, in general. . . . The problem really is with Web sites handing over control of some of their content to third parties."[119]

By avoiding the major technology companies, however, websites using direct sales have to come up with their own quality control processes, which can be subverted in some cases.[120] One example is the *New York Times* website's front-page malware attack of 2009.

In September 2009, the *New York Times* sold advertising space on its website using both third-party ad networks and direct sales. An advertiser claiming to represent the Internet telephony company Vonage contacted the *New York Times* offering to purchase advertising space on NYTimes.com.[121] Vonage had previously run advertisements through the *New York Times*, so the newspaper allowed a third-party vendor it was unfamiliar with to actually deliver the ad. For several weeks, the advertiser submitted wholly legitimate-looking advertisements, which the *New York Times* ran without incident.[122] Then, at the beginning of a weekend, the advertiser replaced the Vonage advertisements with an ad proclaiming that the user's computer was not safe, and that the user should purchase fake antivirus software to protect her computer.[123] That fake antivirus software, once placed on a user's computer, could steal personal data and extort money from consumers hoping to make the virus go away.[124]

The *New York Times* is not the only company victimized by fraudulent advertisers. It is not even the only newspaper that has experienced this type of incident. The website of the *San Francisco Chronicle* (SFGate.com) suffered a similar attack on the same weekend in 2009 as the *New York Times*. One common attack method is to generate an email address that is close or identical to the name of a well-known company and then contact a website claiming to represent that company. Cybercriminals routinely inject malware in that manner, posing as legitimate companies such as Lexus.[125] The online music service Spotify was hit with a malicious advertisement within its desktop program in 2011.[126] User's computers were affected without having to click on any advertisements, and the event led Spotify to shut off all advertising for third parties until it could identify the source of the problem.[127]

These examples illustrate how the infrastructure of online advertising can be subverted for malicious purposes even when the ad networks are not involved. Additional oversight is required in order to validate the identities of would-be advertisers. In many cases, unfortunately, that sort of examination is either not performed, or it is performed in only the most perfunctory manner.

7. First-Party Websites' Cookie Usage Depends Heavily on Extent to Which Online Traffic is the Website's Sole Source of Profit

Companies that primarily provide free content on the Internet logically must find alternative ways of generating revenue. Selling advertising space is the obvious solution, and the more targeted those advertisements are, the more advertisers will pay.[128] The placement of cookies and other tracking mechanisms thus becomes more important for websites dependent on advertising. The online advertising industry is teeming with data brokers willing to pay for the right to retrieve information from cookies.[129]

Using Disconnect, an application which detects when a user's browser is directed to a third-party server (the necessary step to placing or retrieving a third-party cookie), the Subcommittee examined a number of websites to determine the number of third-party servers involved when a consumer visits a particular website. The number of calls to third-party servers varied significantly from site to site. It also varied significantly within the same website, depending on the particular page visited or time of day.[130] However, based on Subcommittee analysis, broad trends emerged. The Subcommittee has observed that websites offering free content tended to have a great number of third-party server calls than websites offering goods or services. These relationships with third parties are potentially a large source of revenue for high traffic websites.

For example, a visit to the website of TDBank, a consumer bank, led to only 11 calls to third-party servers:

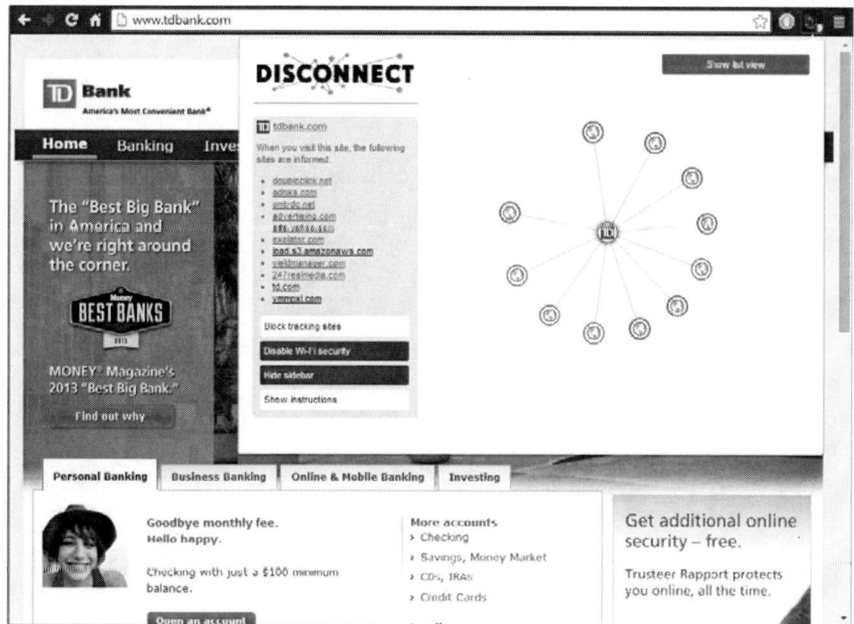

Figure 9. A screenshot of TDBank.com with the Disconnect display identifying third-party server calls.

Figure 10. A screenshot of TMZ.com with the Disconnect display identifying third-party server calls.

By contrast, a visit to TMZ.com, whose business model is heavily dependent on Internet traffic, yielded *352* calls to third-party servers.[131]

In between those two extremes, ESPN—a dynamic company with a suite of business, including activities based on offering free Internet content as well as other cable broadcasting services—had 83 calls to third-party servers.[132]

The Subcommittee observed a similar trend with other websites—the extent to which a company's business model depended on online traffic was a strong predictor of the number of calls to third-party servers. Ford, whose profits derive primarily from its automobile sales, not primarily high Internet traffic, also had 18 calls to third-party servers from its website.[133] The Drudge Report, a solely Internet-based news site, had 326 calls to third-party servers.[134] Bank of America had 11 third-party server calls. AT&T had 32 calls to third-party servers.[135] Senate.gov, the website of the U.S. Senate, had no third-party server calls.[136] Wikipedia, wholly dependent on donations from visitors instead of advertising, also had no third-party server calls. Amazon.com, which takes in revenue from sales of goods, had only a single third-party server call.[137]

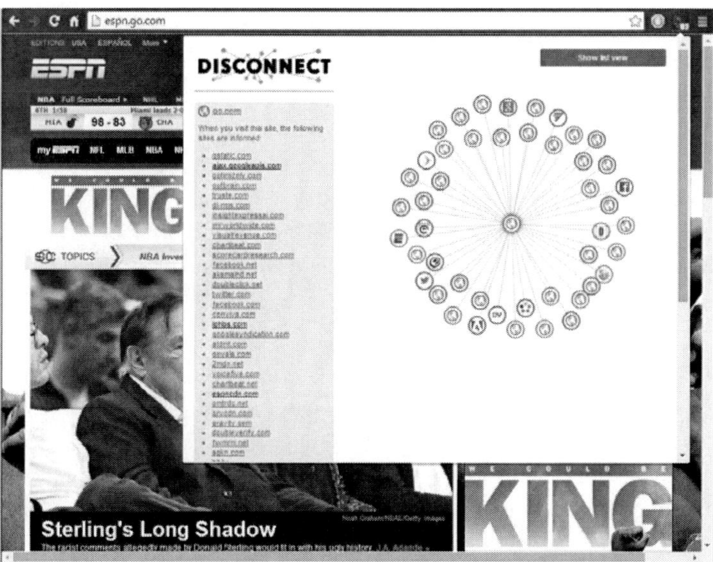

Figure 11. A screenshot of ESPN.com with the Disconnect display identifying third-party server calls.

The results of the Subcommittee's survey suggest a basic problem: data is valuable, and the more a website depends on traffic rather than non-Internet-based revenue, the more it seems to be willing to forge relationships with third parties that may pay to collect that data. As Internet-based companies become a greater portion of the economy, one could reasonably expect that sales of data to third parties will only increase further.

b. Current Online Advertising Regulatory Authorities Do Not Adequately Address Security Concerns in Advertising

Congress has not enacted comprehensive data-security legislation to guide industry standards and establish enforcement benchmarks for federal enforcement agencies to follow. Instead, the Federal Trade Commission (FTC) has regulated the online advertising industry primarily under its authority found in Section 5 of the Federal Trade Commission Act ("FTC Act").[138] Under Section 5 of the FTC Act, the FTC is empowered to begin enforcement actions, levy fines, and seek injunctions against companies that engage in "unfair" or "deceptive" practices.[139]

Following an investigation, the FTC has the authority to initiate an enforcement action against a company if it has "reason to believe" that the law has been violated.[140] The legislative history indicates that Congress intentionally used the general terms of "unfair" and "deceptive" because it believed that providing a list of unfair or deceptive practices would have inevitably left loopholes susceptible to easy evasion.[141] Thus, the FTC was given the task of determining and identifying unfair or deceptive practices through notice and comment rulemaking, on-the- record adjudication, and policy statements.

1. Deceptive Practices Enforcement

To date, the FTC has brought several deceptive practices cases against companies involved in online advertising. However, that enforcement authority essentially requires that a company publicly state a policy that is contradicted by its actions. Thus, FTC deceptive practices enforcement in the online advertising industry has stopped a few clear violations, but has not meaningfully changed what practices are generally considered acceptable.

An act or practice is deceptive when there is (1) representation, omission, or practice, which misleads or is likely to mislead the consumer; (2) a consumer's interpretation of the representation, omission, or practice is considered reasonable under the circumstances; and (3) the misleading representation, omission, or practice is material.[142]

The most prominent FTC deceptive practices enforcement action to date involving the online advertising industry was against Google. In August 2012, Google agreed to pay a record $22.5 million civil penalty to settle FTC charges that it misrepresented its cookie and targeted- advertising practices to users of Apple Inc.'s Safari Internet browser.[143]

The FTC alleged that Google placed tracking cookies on Safari users who visited websites within Google's DoubleClick ad network. Google had previously told these users that they were automatically opted out from a Google tracking cookie because the default settings on the Safari browser blocked third party cookies. Google further represented that as a member of the self-regulatory organization, the Network Advertising Initiative, it was required to disclose its data collection and use practices. The FTC alleged that despite these promises, Google exploited a loophole in Safari's default setting to place a temporary DoubleClick cookie on user's computers. The initial tracking cookie, in turn, allowed additional tracking cookies from DoubleClick—including advertising tracking cookies that Google represented would be blocked from Safari browsers—to track user's Internet activities.[144]

The FTC referred the matter to the Department of Justice on August 8, 2012 which then filed the complaint in the United States District Court for the District of Northern California in San Francisco.[145] District Judge Susan Illston approved the $22.5 million settlement agreement between the two parties on November 17, 2012.[146]

That settlement came after an October 2011 deceptive practices settlement that resolved charges that Google failed to follow its privacy promises when it launched its social network, Google Buzz. The settlement forced Google to implement a privacy program for Google Buzz, submit to FTC audits and reporting for 20 years and face $16,000 fines for any future privacy misrepresentations.[147]

While the FTC's enforcement actions against Google were among its most prominent, other deceptive practices enforcement actions have been levied against smaller companies. In March 2011, the Commission brought a deceptive practice action against the online advertising company, Chitika, Inc., alleging that it placed tracking cookies on consumers' browsers after they opted out of receiving targeted advertisements.

Chitika is an online ad network that engages in behavioral advertising. It uses cookies to track consumers' browsing activities online to serve them targeted advertisements based on that individual's Internet activity. When a consumer visits a website within Chitika's network of publishers, Chitika sets a new cookie or receives information from its tracking cookie that has already been imbedded on the user's browser.[148] The Chitika tracking cookie contains a unique identification number that allows the company to connect an Internet user's activity to a particular computer.[149] Each time a Chitika sets a new tracking cookie or receives information from a previously-placed tracking cookie, the company receives more information on the user to tailor advertisements to that particular user.[150] So long as a consumer visits a website in the Chitika network from the same browser on the same computer at least once a year, the consumer will indefinitely retain the Chitika tracking cookie on her browser.[151] Chitika's network consists of over 350,000 publishers and the information gathered within it helps the service of over 4 billion targeted ads per month.[152]

Internet users have the ability to "opt-out" of having Chitika tracking cookies placed on their browsers. When a user opts out, Chitika sets an "opt-out cookie" in the user's browser and when a user visits a website within Chitika's network, Chitika receives the opt-out cookie and does not place any subsequent tracking cookies on the user's browser. It also does not add any additional information to a previously set Chitika cookie or use the data from the cookie to target advertisements to the consumer. Chitika did not indicate how long the opt-out would last if a user opted out.

The FTC alleged that between May 2008 and February 2010, Chitika delivered opt-out cookies that automatically expired after ten days.[153] After the ten days expired, Chitika placed tracking cookies back on consumers' browsers who had opted out and targeted ads to them again. The Commission alleged that Chitika's claims about its opt-out mechanism were "deceptive" within the meaning of Section 5.

Chitika settled its case with the Commission. The settlement agreement required Chitika to display a clear notice on their website explaining that it collects consumer data and offers an opt-out function.[154] It also prohibited Chitika from selling or transferring consumer data obtained prior to March 1, 2010 and ordered the company to permanently delete all information stored in Chitika user's cookies and all IP addresses collected while it employed a defective opt- out system.[155] Moreover, the agreement required that every targeted ad include a hyperlink that takes the consumer to a clear opt-out mechanism that allows the user to opt out for at least five years.[156] The order subjected Chitika to five years of FTC monitoring to ensure Chitika's compliance with the consent decree.[157]

One other example of the FTC's deceptive practice enforcement against the online advertising industry came in November 2011, when the FTC settled with the online advertiser, ScanScout. ScanScout is a video ad network that acts as an intermediary between publishers and advertisers. It engages in behavioral advertising, collecting information about consumers' online activities and to serve targeted ads based on the user's interest. The FTC alleged that from April 2007 to September 2009, ScanScout used Flash cookies to collect and store user data in its efforts to facilitate the behavioral targeting of video advertisements.[158] Flash cookies are not controlled through a computer's browser, so if a user tries to change her browsers' privacy settings to delete or block cookies, Flash cookies remain unaffected.[159] Since browsers could not block Flash cookies, users could not prevent ScanScout from collecting data on their Internet activities or from serving them targeted video advertisements.

From April 2007 until September 2009, ScanScout's privacy policy on its website stated in pertinent part, "[Users] can opt out of receiving a cookie by changing your browser settings to prevent the receipt of cookies."[160] The FTC alleged that this false statement constituted a deceptive act or practice in or affecting commerce in violation of Section 5.[161]

The FTC and ScanScout entered into a settlement agreement on November 8, 2011, which was finalized on December 21, 2011. The settlement required ScanScout to host a notice on its website that read, "We collect information about your activities on certain websites to send you targeted ads. To opt out of our targeted advertisements click here."[162] When selected, the hyperlink takes consumers directly to an opt-out mechanism that allows them to prevent ScanScout from collecting information that can identify them or their computer; redirecting the user's browser to third parties that collect data without their approval; and associating any previously collected data with the user.[163] As part of the settlement, ScanScout submitted to five years of FTC monitoring for compliance with the order.

2. Unfair Practices Enforcement

To date, the FTC has not brought unfair practices enforcement actions against companies in the online advertising industry. That absence of enforcement largely reflects the lack of clear standards of conduct within the industry itself. FTC standards for unfair practice depend heavily on industry common practice and the standards set by self-regulatory bodies.

FTC officials informed the Subcommittee that an act or practice is unfair when it: (1) causes or is likely to cause substantial injury to consumers; (2) cannot be reasonably avoided by consumers; and (3) is not outweighed by countervailing benefits to consumers or to competition.[164] Industry standards and self-regulatory guidelines weigh heavily in the assessment of what constitutes reasonable actions for companies in a given industry.

3. FTC Enforcement Actions Against Online Advertisers under Other Statutes

The FTC's authority to regulate online advertising under other statutes tends to be for very specific types of data. The most prominent examples include:

- the Children's Online Privacy Protection Act (COPPA),[165]
- the Fair Credit Reporting Act,[166]
- the Gramm-Leach-Bliley Act,[167]
- the Health Insurance Portability and Accountability Act of 1996,[168]
- the Cable Television Consumer Protection and Competition Act,[169] and
- the Health Information Technology for Economic and Clinical Health Act.[170]

One specific enforcement action in the online advertising arena was brought under COPPA. That law was enacted in 1998 to protect the safety and privacy of children using the Internet. The legislation prohibits the unauthorized or unnecessary collection of children's personal information online by operators of Internet websites or online services. The Commission promulgated regulations that applied to any "operator" of a website directed at children that has knowledge that it is collecting or maintaining children's personal information.[171] The FTC's rule under COPPA requires that website operators notify parents and obtain their consent before they collect, use, or disclose personal information from children under 13. The rule also requires that website operators post a privacy policy that is clear, understandable, and complete for users to read.

On March 26, 2012, the FTC filed an action in the United States District Court for the Northern District against RockYou, Inc., alleging that RockYou violated the FTC's COPPA rule. RockYou is a social game website where users could play games and use the site to upload photos from their computers or web, add captions, and choose music to create a slideshow.[172] Users were required to register with RockYou, using an email address and password, if they wanted to save or edit their slideshows. Registrants were also required to enter a birth year, gender, zip code and country with their registration.[173] RockYou stored the email addresses and passwords in their internal database.

The Commission alleged that from December 2008 through January 2010, RockYou accepted approximately 179,000 registrations from children under the age of 13 without parent consent.[174] Since the website asked for registrant's date of birth and other personal information, RockYou fell within the FTC's definition of operator under the rule and it put children's personal information at risk because the slideshows that the children created could be shared online. Specifically, the FTC charged that RockYou violated the COPPA rule by: (1) failing to spell out its collection, use and disclosure policy for children's information; (2) failing to obtain verifiable parental consent before collecting children's personal information; and (3) failing to maintain reasonable procedures to protect the confidentiality, security, and integrity of personal information collected from children.[175]

RockYou and the FTC entered into a consent agreement and settlement order on March 27, 2012.[176] The consent decree enjoined RockYou from future collection of information from children online and forced the company to delete the information it had already collected in violation of the COPPA rule.[177] Moreover, the FTC fined RockYou $250,000 and ordered the company to post a link to the Commission's consumer education website on its own website for five years.[178] Finally, the settlement required RockYou to implement a data security program, submit compliance reports to the Commission allow security audits by independent third-party auditors every other year for 20 years.[179]

4. The FTC's 2010 Proposed Regulatory Framework

The FTC proposed a regulatory framework in December 2010 that noted several of the most pressing consumer hazards in the online advertising industry. That report cast strong doubt on the FTC's "notice-and-choice model," under which companies can avoid enforcement action so long as their privacy policies gave notice to consumers, who could then make an informed choice about whether to use a particular Internet service.[180] The FTC noted that "the notice-and- choice model, as implemented, has led to long, incomprehensible privacy policies that consumers typically do not read, let alone understand."[181] Given the FTC's criticism of the model it had hitherto used in its enforcement actions, the need for some protection beyond formal notice seemed evident. The framework went on to suggest some basic principles for regulation, and tasked the businesses within the online advertising industry to come up with policies that matched those principles.

c. Incentives to Limit Responsibility for the Harmful Effects of Online Advertising

Many consumers have developed an expectation that web content delivered by reputable sources will be free of dangerous malware. The Subcommittee's investigation has determined that even the most sophisticated advertisers have difficulty guaranteeing consumer security due in part to numerous structural vulnerabilities in the online advertising model. The current state of law and regulation addressing online advertising is sparse, focusing mainly on criminal actors rather than the responsibilities of intermediaries. While still pursuing criminal actors, the responsibility of industry and private stakeholders to implement precautionary measures should be clarified. The current structure leaves consumers with no recourse when they are victim of a malware attack.

1. Ad-Hosting Websites Often Do Not Know What Advertisements Will be Run on Their Website

Websites that run advertisements delivered by ad networks almost never know all of the advertisers that will operate on their website on any given day. While the host websites can request that certain categories of advertisements be excluded (for example, violent or pornographic advertisements), they are often completely unaware of what advertisers end up operating on their websites until after the fact. Consequently, when a malicious advertisement is delivered to a visitor, the host website can plausibly claim that it had no idea of the danger.

2. Ad Networks do not Control the Advertisement Creative Directly

As discussed above, ad networks—among the most sophisticated technology companies in the world—generally do not have direct control over the advertisements they deliver. Because such control would incur bandwidth costs and slow delivery, there is a clear disincentive to retain control over the advertisement's content. While there are reputational costs associated with malware attacks through ad networks, such costs are only realized if the attack is (a) detected and (b) linked to an advertisement delivered by that ad network. It is difficult for an ordinary consumer to even identify why, or even if, her computer has been compromised. Learning how and from what entity she acquired the malware in question is a near impossibility for the average consumer.

3. Self-Regulatory Groups do not Provide Sufficient Oversight on Security and Privacy issues

The online advertising industry self-regulatory groups are not currently stand-ins for comprehensive regulators. While they do generate codes and provide enforcement for privacy standards, they could improve their practices by expelling or publicly identifying members who are not in compliance with their codes. Industry participants should also expand their self- regulatory efforts into the security realm. While self-regulatory bodies have, in the privacy context, promulgated standards and rules, there have not been any similarly enforced standards regarding the threat from online advertising malware attacks. One industry effort to address security foundered reportedly due to members of the industry "desiring to refocus their resources on aggressively defending industry practices to policy groups and regulatory bodies."[182] New efforts, such as the recently launched Trust in Ads initiative, should strive to issue meaningful security standards to protect consumers.

End Notes

[1] Press Release, Interactive Advertising Bureau, 2013 Internet ad Revenues Soar to $42.8 billion, Hitting Landmark High & Surpassing Broadcast Television For First Time—Marks 17% Rise Over Record-Setting Revenues in 2012 (Apr. 10, 2014) http://www.iab.net/about_the_iab/recent_press_releases/press_release_archive/press_release/pr-041014.

[2] J. Howard Beales and Jeffrey Eisenach, *An Empirical Analysis Of The Value Of Information Sharing in the Market for Online Content*, Navigant Economics, 2014, https://www.aboutads.info/resource/fullvalueinfostudy.pdf.

[3] *Id.*

[4] Written Testimony of Craig D. Spiezle before the Senate Committee on Homeland Security & Government Affairs Permanent Subcommittee on Investigations, May 15, 2014.

[5] Leelin Thye, *"Danger: Malware Ahead!-Please, Not My Site"*, SYMANTEC (Jan. 17, 2013), http://www.symantec.com/connect/blogs/danger-malware-ahead-please-not-my-site.

[6] White Paper, *"The Link Between Pirated Software and Cybersecurity Breaches, How Malware in Pirated Software is Costing the World Billions"* (Mar., 2014), http://www.microsoft.com/en- us/news/downloads/presskits/dcu/docs/idc_031814.pdf.

[7] Cisco, *"2013 Annual Security Report"* (2013), https://www.cisco.com/web/offer/gist_ty2_asset/Cisco_2013_ASR.pdf.

[8] See, e.g. Commercial Privacy Bill of Rights Act of 2011 S. 799, 112th Cong. (2011).

[9] As opposed to, for example, the Health Insurance Portability and Accountability Act's Privacy Rule for health information.

[10] Press Release, The White House, We Can't Wait: Obama Administration Unveils Blueprint for a "Privacy Bill of Rights" to Protect Consumers Online (February 23, 2012) http://www.whitehouse.gov/the-press-office/2012/02/23/we-can-t-wait-obama-administration-unveils-blueprint-privacy-bill-rights.

[11] David Goldman, *Do Not Track proposal is DOA*, CNN (July 16, 2013), http:// money.cnn.com/2013/07/16/technology/do-not-track/.

[12] Edward Moyer, *Yahoo says malware attack farther reaching than thought*, CNET (Jan. 11, 2014), http://www.cnet.com/news/yahoo-says-malware-attack-farther-reaching-than-thought/; Lance Whitney, *Yahoo malware turned PCs into Bitcoin miners*, CNET (Jan. 9, 2014), http://news.cnet.com/8301-1009_3-57616958-83/yahoo-malware-turned-pcs-into-bitcoin-miners/

[13] Whitney, *supra.*

[14] Interview with Yahoo, in Wash., D.C. (Jan. 16, 2014).

[15] Alex Hern, *Yahoo malware turned European Computers into bitcoin slaves*, THE GUARDIAN (Jan. 8, 2014), http://www.theguardian.com/technology/2014/jan/08/yahoo-malware-turned-europeans-computers-into-bitcoin-slaves.

[16] McEnroe Navaraj, *The Wild Wild Web: YouTube ads serving malware*, BROMIUM LABS CALL OF THE WILD BLOG (Feb. 21, 2014), http://labs.bromium.com/2014/02/21/the-wild-wild-web-youtube-ads-serving-malware.

[17] *Id.*

[18] For instance, Yahoo, Google, and Microsoft all operate ad networks.

[19] Subcommittee interview with NAI (Jan. 31, 2014).

[20] *Internet Industry Leaders Offer Tips for Consumers to Avoid Tech Support Advertising Scams*, TRUSTINADS.ORG BLOG (May 7, 2014), http://blog.trustinads.org/2014/05/internet-industry-leaders-offer-tips.html.

[21] See The Federal Trade Commission Act, 15 U.S.C. §45(a), Section 5 in particular.

[22] Interview with Marc Groman, President and CEO, Network Advertising Initiative, in Wash., D.C. (Jan. 31, 2014).

[23] As opposed to, for example, the Health Insurance Portability and Accountability Act's Privacy Rule for health information.

[24] *See, e.g.*, Network Advertising Initiative, *Understanding Online Advertising: How Does it Work?*, https://www.networkadvertising.org/understanding-online-advertising/how-does-it-work.

[25] *Id.*

[26] The Subcommittee detected third-party activity using the "Disconnect Private Browsing" application on a Chrome web browser. As explained on its website, Disconnect "detects when your browser tries to make a connection to anything other than the site you are visiting." *See* https://disconnect.me/disconnect/faq#what-is-disconnect-private- browsing. According to DoubleClick's website, "DoubleClick sends a cookie to the browser after any impression, click, or other activity that results in a call to the DoubleClick server." Since, in our example, there was a call to DoubleClick's server detected by Disconnect, we can infer that a cookie was placed through that interaction.

[27] *See*, Fed. Trade Comm'n., *Cookies: Leaving a Trail on the Web* (Nov. 2011) https://www.consumer.ftc.gov/articles/0042-cookies-leaving-trail-web.

[28] *Id.*

[29] *See, e.g.*, BlueKai, *Privacy Policy*, http://bluekai.com/privacypolicy.php.

[30] The arrangement whereby placing one pixel can allow a third party to place a cookie is called a "pixel tag." *See Id.*

[31] J. Howard Beales and Jeffrey Eisenach, *An Empirical Analysis Of The Value Of Information Sharing in the Market for Online Content*, Navigant Economics, 2014, https://www.aboutads.info/resource/fullvalueinfostudy.pdf.

[32] Charles Arthur, *Why the default settings on your device should be right first time*, THE GUARDIAN (Nov. 30, 2013), http://www.theguardian.com/technology/2013/dec/01/default-settings-change-phones-computers.

[33] Press Release, Fed. Trade Comm'n, Google Will Pay $22.5 Million to Settle FTC Charges It Misrepresented Privacy Assurances to Users of Apple's Safari Internet Browser (Aug. 9, 2013), http://www.ftc.gov/news-events/press-releases/2012/08/google-will-pay-225-million-settle-ftc-charges-it-misrepresented.

[34] James Temple, *Mozilla anticookie tool plans crumbling*, S.F. GATE (Nov. 5, 2013), http://www.sfgate.com/technology/dotcommentary/article/Mozilla-anticookie-tool-plans-crumbling-4958045.php.

[35] *See*, Appnexus, *Ad Tags: an Introduction*, https://wiki.appnexus.com/display/industry/ Ad +Tags.

[36] Interview with Craig Spiezle, Executive Director and President, Online Trust Alliance, in Wash., D.C. (Mar. 19, 2014).

[37] *Id.*

[38] Interview with Mike Zaneis, Executive Vice President, Public Policy and General Counsel, Interactive Advertising Bureau, in Wash., D.C. (Apr. 23, 2014).

[39] CNN (Apr. 27, 2014), http://www.cnn.com. The Subcommittee has not confirmed that this particular sale was direct, but the coordination across different sections of the same website is emblematic of direct sales.

[40] Description of Impressions, GOOGLE, https://support.google.com/adwords/answer/6320?hl=en (last visited May 2, 2014).

[41] White Paper, *Ad Network vs Ad Exchanges: How do they Compare?*, OPENX at 2 (Oct. 3, 2013), http://openx.com/whitepaper/ad-exchange-vs-ad-network-how-do-they-compare (hereinafter "OpenX White Paper").

[42] *Id.*

[43] Video, *The Evolution of Online Display Advertising*, INTERNET ADVERTISING BUREAU UK (Nov. 11, 2012), http://www.iabuk.net/video/the-evolution-of-online-display-advertising.

[44] OpenX White Paper, *supra* note 41 at 2.

[45] Webinar, *Ad Networks vs. Ad Exchanges*, OPENX, http://openx.com/webinars/ad-networks-vs-ad-exchanges.

[46] *Id.*

[47] *Id.*

[48] *Id.*

[49] *Id.*

[50] *Id.*

[51] *Id.*

[52] Video, INTERNET ADVERTISING BUREAU UK, *supra* note 43.

[53] Webinar, OPENX, *supra* note 45.

[54] *Id.*

[55] Video, INTERNET ADVERTISING BUREAU UK, *supra* note 43.

[56] Webinar, OPENX, *supra* note 45.

[57] *Id.*

[58] OpenX White Paper, *supra* note 41 at 5.

[59] *Id.*

[60] *Id.*

[61] *Id.*

[62] Webinar, OPENX, *supra* note 45.

[63] *See*, Michael Johnston, *What Are Average CPM Rates in 2014?*, MONETIZE PROS (Jan. 27, 2014), http://monetizepros.com/blog/2014/average-cpm-rates.

[64] OpenX White Paper, *supra* note 41 at 5.

[65] *Id.*

[66] Webinar, OPENX, *supra* note 45.

[67] *Id.*

[68] *Id.*

[69] *Id.*

[70] J. Howard Beales and Jeffrey Eisenach, *An Empirical Analysis Of The Value Of Information Sharing in the Market for Online Content*, NAVIGANT ECONOMICS, 2014, https://www.aboutads.info/resource/fullvalueinfostudy.pdf.

[71] Webinar, OPENX, *supra* note 45.

[72] In an interview with the Subcommittee, NAI noted that while consumers have ability to comment on proposed rule changes, ultimate approval authority feel to NAI's Board of Directors, comprised of industry representatives. IAB also told the Subcommittee that consumers have a limited role in their rulemaking process. Interview with Marc Groman, President and CEO, Network Advertising Initiative, in Wash., D.C. (Jan. 31, 2014).

[73] Fed. Trade. Comm'n., PROTECTING CONSUMER PRIVACY IN AN ERA OF RAPID CHANGE, at 68 (Mar. 2012), http://www.ftc.gov/sites/default/files/documents/reports/federal-trade-commission-report-protecting-consumer-   privacy-era-rapid-change-recommendations/120326privacyreport.pdf (hereinafter "FTC 2012 Privacy Report").

[74] *Id.*

[75] Majority Staff of S. Comm. on Commerce, Science, and Transportation, A REVIEW OF THE DATA BROKER INDUSTRY: COLLECTION, USE, AND SALE OF CONSUMER DATE FOR MARKETING PURPOSES, (Dec. 2013), http://op.bna.com/der.nsf/id/sbay-9ehtxt/$File/Rockefeller%20report%20on%20data%20brokers.pdf   (hereinafter   "Sen.   Commerce Committee Data Broker Report").

[76] *Id* at ii.

[77] *Id.*

[78] *Id* at 30.

[79] *Id* at iii.

[80] McEnroe Navaraj, *The Wild Wild Web: YouTube ads serving malware*, BROMIUM LABS CALL OF THE WILD BLOG (Feb. 21, 2014), http://labs.bromium.com/2014/02/21/the-wild-wild-web-youtube-ads-serving-malware.

[81] *Id.*

[82] *Id.*

[83] *Id.*

[84] Interview with Google in Wash., D.C (May 12, 2014).

[85] The Subcommittee did not speak with Major League Baseball and based its analysis on expert testimony and publicly available information.

[86] Evan Keiser, *MLB.com distributing Fake AV Malware via compromised Ad Network*, SILVERSKY ALTITUDE BLOG (Jun. 18, 2012), https://www.silversky.com/blog/mlbcom-distributing -fake-av-malware-compromised-ad-network.

[87] Dan Raywood, *Major League Baseball website hit by malvertising that may potentially impact 300,000 users*, SC MAGAZINE UK (Jun. 20, 2012), http://www.scmagazineuk.com/major-league-baseball-website-hit-by-malvertising-that-may-potentially-impact-300000-users/article/246503.

[88] Fahmida Y. Rashid, *MLB.com Serving Fake Antivirus Via Malicious Online Ads*, SECURITY WATCH (Jun. 19, 2012), http://securitywatch.pcmag.com/none/299326-mlb-com-serving-fake-antivirus-via-malicious-online-ads.

[89] Keiser, *supra* note 86.

[90] *Id.*

[91] Interview with Craig Spiezle, Executive Director and President, Online Trust Alliance, in Wash., D.C. (Mar. 19, 2014).

[92] Yahoo provided the Subcommittee with a detailed briefing concerning the causes of the breach and company's response. The Subcommittee relied on public information when summarizing the event in order to protect Yahoo's confidential security practices.

[93] Faith Karimi and Joe Sutton, *Malware attack hits thousands of Yahoo users per hour*, CNN (Jan. 6, 2014), http://www.cnn.com/2014/01/05/tech/yahoo-malware-attack.

[94] Chris Smith, *Yahoo ad malware attack far greater than anticipated*, YAHOO NEWS (Jan. 13, 2014), http://news.yahoo.com/yahoo-ad-malware-attack-far-greater-anticipated-114523608.html.

[95] Interview with Yahoo, in Wash., D.C. (Jan. 16, 2014).

[96] Chris Smith, *Yahoo ad malware hijacked computers for Bitcoin mining*, BGR (Jan. 9, 2014), http://bgr.com/2014/01/09/yahoo-malware-bitcoin-mining.

[97] Interview with Yahoo, in Wash., D.C. (Jan. 16, 2014).

[98] Karimi and Sutton, *supra* note 93.

[99] *Id.*

[100] The attack targeted Windows users with non-updated version of Java.

[101] *Id.*

[102] Interview with Alex Stamos, Yahoo, in Wash., D.C. (May 12, 2014).

[103] Interview with Craig Spiezle, Executive Director and President, Online Trust Alliance, in Wash., D.C. (Mar. 19, 2014).

[104] Elinor Mills, *Malware delivered by Yahoo, Fox, Google ads*, CNET (Mar. 22, 2010), http://www.cnet.com/news/malware-delivered-by-yahoo-fox-google-ads.

[105] *Id.*

[106] *Id.*

[107] *Id.*

[108] *Id.*

[109] *Id.*

[110] *See, e.g.*, Turn, Inc. "Social Responsibility", ("As an industry leader, Turn participates actively in industry groups—IAB, DAA, and NAI—that are establishing safety mechanisms, implementing best practices, and enforcing guidelines to safeguard consumer privacy."), http://www.turn.com/company/social-responsibility.

[111] Complaint, *In the Matter of Epic Marketplace, Inc. et al.*, No. C-4389 (Mar. 13, 2013), http://www.ftc.gov/sites/default/files/documents/cases/2013/03/130315epicmarketplacecmpt.pdf.

[112] *Id.* at 2.

[113] *Id.*

[114] Jonathan Mayer, *Tracking the Trackers: To Catch a History Thief*, THE CENTER FOR INTERNET AND SOCIETY, STANFORD LAW SCHOOL (July 19, 2011), http://cyberlaw.stanford.edu/node/6695.

[115] Press Release, Fed. Trade Comm'n, FTC Approves Final Order Settling Charges Against Epic Marketplace, Inc. (Mar. 19, 2013), http://www.ftc.gov/news-events/press-releases/2013/03/ftc-approves-final-order-settling-charges- against-epic. The terms of the settlement barred further violations and imposed a $16,000 penalty for any violations of the consent decree.

[116] NAI Compliance, *An Update on NAI Compliance*, NETWORK ADVERTISING INITIATIVE COMPLIANCE BLOG (Oct. 20, 2011), https://www.networkadvertising.org/blog/update-nai-compliance.

[117] *Id.*

[118] Network Advertising Initiative, 2013 ANNUAL COMPLIANCE REPORT (2013), http://www.networkadvertising.org/2013_NAI_Compliance_Report.pdf.

[119] Elinor Mills, *Ads—the new malware delivery format*, CNET (Sept. 15, 2009), http://www.cnet.com/news/ads-the- new-malware-delivery-format.

[120] The incidents in this section are all drawn from publicly available reports, not interviews with the parties involved.

[121] Ashlee Vance, *Times Web Ads Show Security Breach*, N.Y. TIMES (Sept. 14, 2009), http://www.nytimes.com/2009/09/15/technology/internet/15adco.html?_r=2&.

[122] *Id.*

[123] *Id.*

[124] *Id.*

[125] Mills, *supra* note 119.

[126] Patrik Runald, *Spotify application serves malicious ads*, WEBSENSE (March 25, 2011), http://community.websense.com/blogs/securitylabs/archive/2011/03/25/spotify-application-serves-malicious-ads.aspx.

[127] Spotify, "We've turned off all 3rd party display ads that could have caused it until we find the exact one." (Mar. 25, 2011, 4:44 AM), Tweet, https://twitter.com/Spotify/status/51248179039059968.

[128] Julia Angwin, *The Web's New Gold Mine: Your Secrets*, THE WALL STREET JOURNAL (July 30, 2010), http://online.wsj.com/news/articles/SB10001424052748703940904575395073512989404; see also Bryce Cullinane, *Cookies For Sale? How Websites Obtain Permission to Track and Sell Online User Data*, MIRSKY & COMPANY, PLLC BLOG (Feb. 19, 2013), http://mirskylegal.com/2013/02/how-websites-obtain-permission-to-track-and-sell-online-user-data.

[129] Sen. Commerce Committee Data Broker Report, *supra* note 75.

[130] For example, of the websites tested, none that had more than 100 third-party server calls ever had fewer than 100. Some websites would go as low as 120 third-party server calls on one visit and as high as 1500 at other times. The figures listed in this report are all from specific test visits and are representative of the sites in question. All of the websites listed were checked at the same time of the day and week to correct for any increases in advertising activity to correspond with high or low-traffic times.

[131] TMZ.com. Third-party server activity measured on Apr. 26, 2014.

[132] Espn.go.com. Third-party server activity measured on Apr. 26, 2014.

[133] Ford.com. Third-party server activity measured from a test visit on Apr. 26, 2014.

[134] DrudgeReport.com. Third-party server activity measured from a test visit on Apr. 26, 2014.

[135] BankofAmerica.com. Third-party server activity measured from a test visit on Apr. 26, 2014.

[136] Senate.gov. Third-party server activity measured from a test visit on Apr. 26, 2014.

[137] Amazon.com. Third-party server activity measured from a test visit on Apr. 28, 2014.

[138] 15 U.S.C. § 45.

[139] *Id.*

[140] Fed. Trade Comm'n, *A Brief Overview of the Federal Trade Commission's Investigative and Law Enforcement Authority* (July 2008), http://www.ftc.gov/ogc/brfovrvw.shtm.

[141] See H.R.REP. NO. 63-1142, at 19 (1914) (Conf. Rep.) (observing if Congress "were to adopt the method of definition, it would undertake an endless task").

[142] Interview with Lisa Harrison, General Counsel, Mark Acorn, Privacy, Molly Crawford, Bureau of Consumer Protection, Maneesha Mithal, Associate Director, Privacy and Identity Protection Division, Chris Olsen, Associate Director, Privacy and Identity Protection Division and Kim Vandecar, Congressional Liaison, Fed. Trade Comm'n. in Wash., D.C. (Mar. 21, 2014).

[143] Press Release, Fed. Trade Comm'n, Google Will Pay $22.5 Million to Settle FTC Charges It Misrepresented Privacy Assurances to Users of Apple's Safari Internet Browser (Aug. 9, 2013), http://www.ftc.gov/news-   events/press-releases/2012/08/google-will-pay-225-million-settle-ftc-charges-it-misrepresented.

[144] *Id.*

[145] *United States v. Google Inc.*, 3:12-cv-04177, U.S. District Court, Northern District of California (San Francisco).

[146] Sara Forden and Karen Gullo, *Google Judge Accepts $22.5 Million FTC Privacy Settlement*, BLOOMBERG (Nov. 17, 2012), http://www.bloomberg.com/news/2012-11-17/google-judge-accepts-22-5-million-ftc-privacy- settlement.html.

[147] Agreement Containing Consent Order, *In re Google, Inc.* File No. 102 3136 (Mar. 30, 2011).

[148] Complaint at 2, *In re Chitika, Inc.,* No. C-4324 (June 7, 2011).

[149] *Id.*

[150] *Id.*

[151] *Id.*

[152] Chitika Inc., *About Chitika*, http://chitika.com/about.

[153] Complaint at 3, *In re Chitika, Inc.* No. C-4324 (June 7, 2011).

[154] Decision and Order at 3, *In re Chitika, Inc.*, No. C-4324 (June 7, 2011).

[155] *Id.* at 4.

[156] *Id.*

[157] *Id.* at 5.

[158] Complaint at 2, *In re ScanScout Inc.*, No. C-4344 (Dec. 14, 2011).

[159] *Id.*

[160] *Id.*

[161] *Id.*at 3.

[162] Decision and Order at 3-4, *In re ScanScout Inc.*, No C-4344 (Dec. 14, 2011).

[163] *Id.* at 4.

[164] Interview with Lisa Harrison, General Counsel, Mark Acorn, Privacy, Molly Crawford, Bureau of Consumer Protection, Maneesha Mithal, Associate Director, Privacy and Identity Protection Division, Chris Olsen, Associate Director, Privacy and Identity Protection Division and Kim Vandecar, Congressional Liaison, Fed. Trade Comm'n. in Wash., D.C. (Mar. 21, 2014).

[165] Pub. L. No. 105-277, 112 Stat. 2581-728, codified at 15 U.S.C. § 6501 (requiring covered website operators to establish and maintain procedures to protect the confidentiality and security of data gathered from children).

[166] Pub. L. No. 108-159, 117 Stat. 1953, codified at 15 U.S.C. § 1681 (requiring the FTC and other agencies to develop rules for financial institutions aimed at reducing identity theft against consumers).

[167] Pub. L. No. 106-102, 113 Stat. 1338, codified at 15 U.S.C. § 6801 (instructing the FTC and federal banking agencies to promulgate data-security standards for financial institutions to protect against "unauthorized access to or use of" consumer financial records or information).

[168] Pub. L. No. 104-91, codified at 45 U.S.C. § 1320d (requiring health care providers to maintain security standards for electronically stored health care information).

[169] Pub. L. No. 102-385, 106 Stat. 1460, codified at 42 U.S.C. § 551 (forcing cable companies to enact policies aimed at preventing unauthorized access to certain subscriber information).

[170] Pub. L. No. 111-5, 123 Stat 115, codified at 42 U.S.C. § 17921 (requiring regulated entities to provide notice of unsecured breaches of health care information in particular instances).

[171] 16 C.F.R. Part 312.

[172] Complaint at 4, *United States v. RockYou, Inc.*, (N.D. Cal. filed Mar. 26, 2012), Civil Action No. 12-CV-1487, http://www.ftc.gov/sites/default/files/documents/cases/2012/03/120327 rockyoucmpt.pdf.

[173] *Id.* at 5.

[174] *Id.* at 7.

[175] Press Release, Fed. Trade Comm'n, FTC Charges That Security Flaws in RockYou Game Site Exposed 32 Million Email Addresses and Passwords (Mar. 27, 2012), http://www.ftc.gov/ news-events/press-releases/2012/03/ftc-charges-security-flaws-rockyou-game-site-exposed-32-million.

[176] Consent Decree and Order for Civil Penalties, Injunction and Other Relief, *United States v. RockYou, Inc.*, No. 12-CV-1487, (N.D. Cal. 2012), http://www.ftc.gov/sites/default/files/ documents/cases/2012/03/120327rockyouorder.pdf.

[177] *Id.* at 5-6.

[178] *Id.* at 7.

[179] *Id.* at 9.

[180] Fed. Trade. Comm'n., PROTECTING CONSUMER PRIVACY IN AN ERA OF RAPID CHANGE: A PROPOSED FRAMEWORK FOR BUSINESSES AND POLICYMAKERS, at iii (Dec. 2010), http:// www.ftc.gov/sites/default/files/documents/reports/federal-trade-commission-bureau-consumer-protection-preliminary-ftc-staff-report-protecting-consumer/101201privacy report.pdf.

[181] *Id.*

[182] Written Testimony of Craig D. Spiezle before the Senate Committee on Homeland Security & Government Affairs Permanent Subcommittee on Investigations, May 15, 2014; *see also* Caitlin Condon, *StopBadware steps down as leader of the Ads Integrity Alliance*, STOP BADWARE BLOG (Jan. 20, 2014), https://www.stopbadware.org/blog/2014/01/20/ stopbadware-steps-down-as-leader-of-the-ads-integrity-alliance.

In: Hidden Hazards of Online Advertising
Editor: Lillian Wallace
ISBN: 978-1-63321-458-3
© 2014 Nova Science Publishers, Inc.

Chapter 2

TESTIMONY OF ALEX STAMOS, VICE PRESIDENT OF INFORMATION SECURITY, YAHOO! INC. HEARING ON "ONLINE ADVERTISING AND HIDDEN HAZARDS TO CONSUMER SECURITY AND DATA PRIVACY"[*]

INTRODUCTION

Chairman Levin, Ranking Member McCain, and distinguished members of the subcommittee, thank you for convening this hearing and for inviting me to testify today about security issues relating to online advertising. I appreciate the opportunity to share my thoughts and to discuss the user-first approach to security we take at Yahoo.

My name is Alex Stamos, and I am Yahoo's Vice President of Information Security and Chief Information Security Officer. I joined Yahoo in March. Prior to that I served as Chief Technology Officer of Artemis Internet and co-founded iSEC Partners. I have spent my career building and improving secure, trustworthy systems, and I am very proud to work on security at Yahoo.

---

[*] This is an edited, reformatted and augmented version of testimony presented May 15, 2014 before the Senate Homeland Security and Government Affairs Committee, Permanent Subcommittee on Investigations.

Yahoo is a global technology company that provides personalized products and services, including search, advertising, content, and communications, in more than 45 languages in 60 countries. We strive to make these daily habits inspire and entertain our users. As a pioneer of the World Wide Web, we enjoy some of the longest lasting customer relationships on the web. It is because we never take these relationships for granted that 800 million users each month trust Yahoo to provide them with Internet services across mobile and web.

One reason I joined Yahoo is that from the top down, the company is devoted to protecting users. Building and maintaining trust through secure products is a critical focus for us, and by default all of our products should be secure for *all* of our users across the globe.

Achieving security online is not an end state; it's a constantly evolving challenge that we tackle head on. At Yahoo, we know that our users rely on us to protect their information. We also see security as a partnership; we want to educate our users to be mindful of their own security habits, and we provide intuitive, user-friendly tools and security resources to help them do so.

Malware is an important issue that is a top priority for Yahoo. While distribution of malware through advertising is one part of the equation, it's important to address the entire malware ecosystem and fight it at each phase of its lifecycle. It is also important to address security more broadly across the Internet.

I outline in my testimony below several specific ways Yahoo is fighting criminals and protecting our users, including: focusing on security in the advertising pipeline and sharing threats; leading the fight on email spam; operating a bug bounty program; and working to fully encrypt 100 percent of Yahoo's network traffic.

INTERNET ADVERTISING SECURITY AND THE FIGHT AGAINST MALWARE AND DECEPTIVE ADS

Internet advertising security is an important focus for us. Yahoo has built a highly sophisticated ad quality pipeline to weed out advertising that does not meet our content, privacy or security standards. In January of this year we became aware of malware distributed on Yahoo sites and immediately took action to remove the malware, investigated how malicious creative copy bypassed our controls, and fixed any vulnerabilities we found. The malware impacted users on Microsoft Windows with out-of-date versions of Java, a browser plugin with a history of security issues, and was mostly targeted at European IP addresses. Users on Macs, mobile devices, and users with up-to-date versions of Java, were not affected.

As I mentioned earlier, the malware ecosystem is expansive and complex. Advertising is only one method of distribution, and distribution is only one part of the problem.

Vulnerabilities that allow an attacker to take control of user devices through popular web browsers like Internet Explorer, plugins like Java, office software and operating systems, are large parts of the problem. Malware is also spread by tricking users into affirmatively installing software they believe to be harmless but is, in fact, malicious.

We successfully block the vast majority of malicious or deceptive advertisements with which bad actors attack our network, and we always strive to defeat those who would compromise our customers' security. This means we regularly improve our systems, including continuously diversifying the set of technologies and testing systems to better emulate different user behaviors. Every ad running on Yahoo's sites or on our ad network is inspected using this system, both when they are created and continuously afterward.

Yahoo also strives to keep deceptive advertisements from ever reaching users. For example, our systems prohibit advertisements that look like operating system messages, because such ads often tout false offers or try to trick users into downloading and installing malicious or unnecessary software. Preventing deceptive advertising once required extensive human intervention, which meant slower response times and inconsistent enforcement. Although no system is perfect, we now use sophisticated machine learning and image recognition algorithms to catch deceptive advertisements. This lets us train our systems about the characteristics of deceptive creatives, advertisers and landing sites so we detect and respond to them immediately.

We are also the driving force behind the SafeFrame standard. The SafeFrame mechanism allows ads to properly display on a web page without exposing a user's private information to the advertiser or network. Thanks to widespread adoption, SafeFrame enhances user privacy and security not only in the thriving marketplace of thousands of publishers on Yahoo, but around the Internet.

We also actively work with other companies through our participation in a number of industry groups, including the Interactive Advertising Bureau's (IAB) Ads Integrity Taskforce, which aims to create a higher level of trust, transparency, quality and safety in interactive advertising. We have proudly joined TrustInAds.org, a group of Internet industry leaders that have come together to protect people from malicious online advertisements and deceptive practices. We also participate in groups dedicated to preventing the spread of malware and disrupting the economic lifecycle of cybercriminals, including the Global Forum for Incident Response and Security Teams (FIRST), the Anti-Phishing Working Group, the Underground Economy Forum, the Operations Security Trust Forum (Ops Trust) and the Bay Area Council CSO Forum.

LEADING THE FIGHT ON EMAIL SPAM

While preventing the placement of malicious advertisements is essential, it is only one part of a larger battle. We also fight the rest of the malware lifecycle by improving ways to validate the authenticity of email and by reducing financial incentives to spread malware. Spam is one of the most effective ways malicious actors make money, and Yahoo is leading the fight to eradicate that source of income. For example, one way spammers act is through "email spoofing". The original Internet mail standards did not require that a sender use an accurate "From:" line in an email. Spammers exploit this to send billions of messages a day that feign to be from friends, family members or business associates. These emails are much more likely to bypass spam filters, as they appear to be from trusted correspondents. Spoofed emails can also be used to trick users into giving up usernames and passwords, a technique known generally as "phishing".

Yahoo is helping the Internet industry tackle these issues. Yahoo was the original author of DomainKeys Identified Mail or DKIM, a mechanism that lets mail recipients cryptographically verify the real origin of email. Yahoo freely contributed the intellectual property behind DKIM to the world, and now the standard protects billions of emails between thousands of domains. Building upon the success of DKIM, Yahoo led a coalition of Internet companies, financial institutions and anti-spam groups in creating the Domain-based Message Authentication, Reporting and Conformance or DMARC standard. You can read about this standard and the companies behind it at DMARC.org. DMARC provides domains a way to tell the rest of the Internet what security mechanisms to expect on email they receive and what actions the sender would like to be taken on spoofed messages.

In April of this year, Yahoo became the first major email provider to publish a strict DMARC reject policy. In essence, we asked the rest of the

Internet to drop messages that inaccurately claim to be from yahoo.com users. Since Yahoo made this change another major provider has enabled DMARC reject. We hope that every major email provider will follow our lead and implement this common sense protection against spoofed email. DMARC has reduced spam purported to come from yahoo.com accounts by over 90%. If used broadly, it would target spammers' financial incentives with crippling effectiveness.

INCENTIVIZING SHARING: THE BUG BOUNTY PROGRAM

Part of keeping our users' data secure is building trustworthy products. To this end, Yahoo operates one of the most progressive bug bounty programs on the Internet, details of which can be viewed at bugbounty.yahoo.com. Our bug bounty program encourages security researchers to report possible flaws in our systems to us via a secure web portal. In this portal we engage researchers and discuss their findings. If their bug turns out to be real, we swiftly fix it and reward the reporter with up to $15,000. In an age where security bugs are often auctioned off and then used maliciously, we believe it is critical that we and other companies create an ecosystem where both burgeoning and established security experts are rewarded for reporting, and not exploiting, vulnerabilities.

ENCRYPTION ACROSS YAHOO

Yahoo invests heavily to ensure the security of our users and their data across all of our products. In January, we made encrypted browsing the default for Yahoo Mail. And as of March of this year, domestic and international traffic moving between Yahoo's data centers has been fully encrypted. Our ongoing goal is to enable a secure encrypted experience for *all of our users,* no matter what device they use or from which country they access Yahoo.

CONCLUSION

I want to restate that security online is not, and will never be, an end state. It's a constantly evolving, global challenge that our industry is tackling head on. Threats that stem from the ad pipeline, or elsewhere, are not unique to any one online company or ad network. And while bad actors pose real threats, we are strongly dedicated to staying ahead of them.

Yahoo fights for user security on multiple fronts. We partner with other companies to detect and prevent the spread of malware via advertising and pioneered the SafeFrame standard to assure user privacy in ad serving. We have led the industry in combating spam in phishing with DKIM and DMARC. We continuously improve our product security with the help of the wider research and security communities. Finally, we are the largest media publisher to enable encryption for our users across the world.

Yahoo will continue to innovate in product security. We will continue to integrate secure development practices into our software lifecycle. We will continue to view user trust and security as top priorities.

Thank you for the opportunity to testify.

In: Hidden Hazards of Online Advertising   ISBN: 978-1-63321-458-3
Editor: Lillian Wallace   © 2014 Nova Science Publishers, Inc.

Chapter 3

TESTIMONY OF GEORGE SALEM, SENIOR PRODUCT MANAGER, GOOGLE, INC. HEARING ON "ONLINE ADVERTISING AND HIDDEN HAZARDS TO CONSUMER SECURITY AND DATA PRIVACY"[*]

Chairman Levin, Ranking Member McCain, and Senators of the Subcommittee:

Thank you for the opportunity to testify today on Google's efforts to combat malware on the web. My name is George Salem and, as a Senior Product Manager on our Ads Policy team, I develop tools for and support our teams of engineers who fight abuse on our platforms. These teams work to identify bad sites and malware; specific divisions seek to find the root of the malware and combat malicious advertising, also known as "malvertising."

Ensuring our users' safety and security is one of Google's main objectives. One of the biggest threats consumers face on the web is malicious software, known as malware, that can seek to control computers or software programs. Malware allows malicious actors to make money off of innocent victims in various ways. Infected computers can be used to send email spam, support distributed denial-of-service attacks, or extract sensitive user information for means that include identity theft, which has now topped the list of consumer

---

[*] This is an edited, reformatted and augmented version of testimony presented May 15, 2014 before the Senate Homeland Security and Government Affairs Committee, Permanent Subcommittee on Investigations.

complaints reported to the Federal Trade Commission for thirteen years in a row. Protecting our users against such incursions on their data advances important security and privacy objectives.

Today, I wish to share three main messages:

First, we believe in providing our users the strongest protections against harmful or malicious content. We think about this problem broadly: beyond just malware, we seek to protect our users against any practice that negatively impacts their experience on the web.

Second, we have a two-pronged approach to fighting malware: prevent and disable. Through a combination of sophisticated algorithms and manual review, we prevent users from visiting bad sites and we proactively scan tens of millions of ads each day across multiple platforms and browsers, disabling any ads we find to have malware.

Third, the fight against malware is a team effort, and we collaborate closely with others in the internet community. The online ecosystem is complex and involves many players, particularly when it comes to advertising. Online platforms are in an ever-shifting battle against parties that benefit from malware and are constantly seeking new ways to avoid our detection and enforcement systems. For that reason, we actively contribute best practices, watch lists, and other resources with others to stay ahead of the game.

It's a complex problem, but we are tackling it head on through tools, user education, and community partnerships.

PROTECTING OUR USERS WITH THE STRONGEST PROTECTIONS AGAINST HARMFUL OR MALICIOUS CONTENT

Protecting the security of our users and their data is one of our main priorities at Google. Beyond malware, we work to protect our users against what we call 'badware' more generally. Badware encompasses any software that may not be strictly malicious or fraudulent but nonetheless results in an unwanted user experience. Badware may include "trick to click" ads and unwanted system preference downloads. Our business relies on users' trust and ease when using our services, and our goal is to protect against anything that may negatively impact a user's experience in using the web.

Some cybercriminals attempt to use online advertising to distribute malware, a practice known as malvertising. Possible vectors of attack include malicious code hidden within an ad creative (such as a .swf file), embedded on a webpage, or within software downloads. While most ads are safe and legitimate, some bad actors try to find ways to trick consumers by getting harmful and deceptive ads published on reputable sites, exploiting the fact that advertising space may be syndicated to parties who are not known to a web site owner.

Malvertising derails users' faith in the online ecosystem. Advertising has had a tremendous role in the evolution of the web, bringing more products, tools and information to consumers, often free of charge. It has allowed the web economy to flourish — Internet ad revenues surged to a landmark $20.1 billion in the last quarter and the advertising-supported Internet ecosystem employs a total of 5.1 million Americans. Bad ads are bad for everyone, including Google and our users.

Google has a long history of fighting malware, however it is distributed. Ten years ago, we launched a set of Software Principles to protect the broader web against unwanted programs. These principles are a broad, continually evolving set of guidelines around installation, disclosure, behavior and snooping. They state, for example, that applications should not trick our users into installing them; should make it clear when they are responsible for changes to users' experience; should clearly disclose when they collect or transmit users' personal information, including through an easy to find privacy policy; and should offer easy options for their disabling or removal, should a user desire it. We follow these guidelines with all the products we develop and distribute, and because we strongly believe they are good for the industry and users worldwide, we encourage our current and prospective business partners to adopt them as well.

OUR TWO-PRONGED APPROACH: PREVENT & DISABLE

Malware and badware are a constantly evolving problem. Google has a two-pronged approach to protecting users from malware online: prevent and disable.

Prevent

One of the best ways to insulate users from the dangers of malware is by proactively preventing them from accessing infected sites altogether. To this end, we developed a tool called Safe Browsing to identify unsafe websites. Safe Browsing creates a continuously updated list of known phishing sites — sites that pretend to be legitimate while trying to trick users into typing in their username and password or sharing other private information — and malware sites. Any page a user visits, as well as all the resources on that page — including pictures and scripts — are checked against this list. Malicious sites we find are then clearly and conspicuously identified as dangerous in Google Search results.

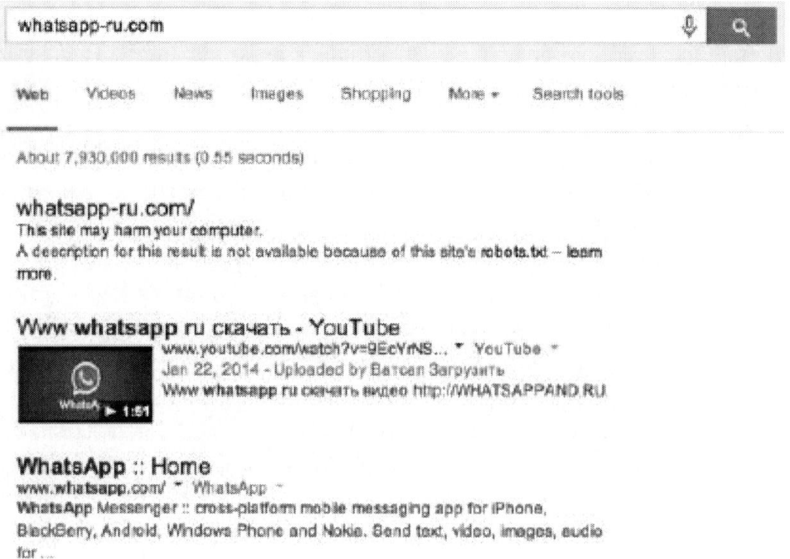

We were the first major search engine to provide this type of warning in search results in 2006, and over a billion people use Safe Browsing today. *Every day*, we examine *billions* of URLs, we discover more than 10,000 new dangerous websites, and we show clear and conspicuous warnings on up to 14 million Google search results and 300,000 malicious downloads.

We help tens of millions of people every week protect themselves from harm by making safe browsing the default setting to users of Google Chrome, Mozilla Firefox and Apple Safari browsers and when users attempt to navigate to a site that would steal their personal information or install software designed to take over their computers they get a warning. Whether a user navigates directly to a compromised site or is directed to it through other means, such as an advertisement, they will instead see an unambiguous interstitial — a page inserted before the user's intended destination site loads — alerting them to the presence of malicious content and advising them to click away from that site. We want to help protect all Internet users, not just those using Google services.

We not only make Safe Browsing data and lists available for others to use for free, but we also provide an interface for others to plug in and review identified malware: our Safe Browsing API. An API is an application programming interface that details how certain software should work together. This API enables client applications to check website addresses against Google's constantly updated list of suspected phishing and malware sites, extending Safe Browsing protection to tens of millions of people every week.

We learned from our Safe Browsing data that most sites containing malicious code have been compromised by malware authors without the knowledge of the webmaster. Consequently, we encourage webmasters to sign up with Google's Webmaster Tools so they can receive notifications when we find security problems on their site. We send thousands of notifications to webmasters every day and provide them with resources to help them fix their issues. Once notified, most of them take action to clean up their sites within 30 days.

In addition, Safe Browsing Alerts for Network Administrators allow Autonomous System (AS) owners to receive early notifications for malicious content found on their networks. A single network or ISP can host hundreds or thousands of different websites. Although network administrators may not be responsible for running the websites themselves, they have an interest in the quality of the content being hosted on their networks. With this additional level of information, administrators can help make the Internet safer by working with webmasters to remove malicious content and fix security vulnerabilities.

Disable

While we work very hard to prevent users from coming into contact with malware on the web in general, we work just as hard to disable and keep malware out of our advertising products and services. We have always prohibited malware in our ads and we have strict suspension policies for partners that spread malware or badware. When an account is suspended, we stop running ads related to that account and we may also suspend any related accounts. We do allow advertisers to appeal a suspension if they fix the violations in the account and send us a report of the changes they have made. For those who we have found to repeatedly violate our policies or who have not resolved their violations, the account will be permanently suspended along with any new account setups the advertiser tries to create in the future.

In 2006, to fight the proliferation of malvertising, we built a dedicated system to scan our Ads platforms and disable any account that distributes malware or badware. Today, we proactively scan <u>billions</u> of ads for malware on all aspects of our advertising services, which includes search and display ads on multiple platforms and browsers. We subsequently re-scan the ads that pose greatest risk to our users to make sure malware has not been introduced into an advertisement after our initial vetting. It should be noted that the vast majority of ads served by Google are good, and most of the ads we disable are hosted by third parties.

Our internal systems have a proven track record in disabling malvertising. In 2013, we disabled more than 350 million bad ads, disapproved more than three million applications from joining our networks due to possible malware, blacklisted more than 200,000 publishers, banned over 270,000 advertisers, and disabled advertising from more than 400,000 websites hiding malware. In fact, we disabled 400,000 ads in the last 30 days for malware policy violations.

While we are very proactive in our efforts against malware, we are often silent to the public about our internal scanning technologies and other specific initiatives. Malware and badware are pushed by bad actors who are sophisticated and dynamic, constantly seeking ways to avoid detection and enforcement by internet platforms. Our goal is to stay one step ahead of malvertisers and not tip them off to our activities even as we share tips and best practices with our users and with the broader Internet community.

We work very hard to prevent malware in our system, but bad actors are very sophisticated and sometimes incidents of malvertising do occur. In 2010, a malware threat called JS:Prontexi was widely publicized. This was one of the first published accounts where an advertising malware threat occurred with no user interaction or clicks. What was not publicized was that Google had become aware of the issue and moved quickly before the reports made it to press. By that time, we were actively scrubbing existing and new ads, already disabling over 10,000 bad ads. The remaining few hundred malware distributing ads were found quickly thereafter.

Earlier this year, a rogue advertiser began serving malware infected ads to users in YouTube. Like many attacks, this began on a Friday afternoon. Days earlier, we had disabled the malware serving site with Safe Browsing. So users of browsers that subscribe to safe browsing - Chrome, Firefox, and Safari - were protected when the attack began. Bromium, the operation publishing the threat, worked with Google directly to identify the exact ads. Since this attack, our teams took the appropriate steps to resolve the issue and beefed up our dynamic tests to prevent such events from occurring again. These are a good examples where like-minded industry partners worked together, behind the scenes, to protect all of our users.

WE WORK WITH INDUSTRY AND SHARE BEST PRACTICES

The anti-malware teams at Google study malware distribution and work closely with the security community to identify malware on the web and share the information more broadly.

To further disseminate helpful information on how to protect users' security, last year we incorporated data on Safe Browsing into our Transparency Report. The site provides information on how many people see Safe Browsing warnings each week, where malicious sites are hosted around the world, how quickly websites become reinfected after their owners clean malware from their sites, and additional information. By providing details about the threats we detect and the warnings we show, we hope to shine some light on the state of web security and encourage safer web security practices.

We are a member of StopBadware.org, an anti-malware nonprofit organization run by the Berkman Center at Harvard Law School that offers resources for website owners, security experts and ordinary users. The site hosts the Search Badware Website Clearinghouse, a searchable database of badware URLs that is voluntarily submitted by StopBadware's partners, sponsors, and users. StopBadware uses the data to analyze and report trends in web-based infections, provide the public with research tools such as the Top 50 Networks list, and assist web hosting companies and other network providers with identifying badware sites on their networks.

We also own VirusTotal, a free web service that provides checks for viruses, worms, trojans and other kinds of malicious content. It uses 51 anti-virus products and scan engines to evaluate user-uploaded files or URLs, and it also offers a free public API. While the service helps identify malicious content, it may also be used as a means to spot false positives — innocuous resources detected as malicious by one or more scanners.

Furthermore, we created an email alias connecting vetted industry players and we use it to notify them directly of malware compromises and trends. Parties on the alias include the anti-malvertising teams from various ad-serving and tech companies. Additionally, we have industry contacts within companies that utilize Google ad products to provide direct feedback.

In 2009 we created Anti-Malvertising.com, a website that provides best practices and investigative resources for publishers and ad operations teams, as well as tips for users. The site includes a custom search engine to run quick background checks on advertisers: one can enter an advertiser's name, company name, or ad URL and access information to help determine whether said advertiser is trustworthy. Anti-Malvertising.com fits into our broader goal to help and encourage all members of the online advertising ecosystem to take an active role in malvertising prevention. It's one part of Google's commitment to educating our customers, improving the industry as a whole, and making the Internet a safer place for everyone.

More recently, we co-founded the Trust in Ads group with Facebook, Twitter and AOL to protect users from malicious online advertisements and deceptive practices. We kicked off this effort by identifying abusive practices in the tech support advertising space. Scam advertisers often present themselves as official representatives of companies of products for which users seek support. Under the disguise of paid assistance, these advertisers trick users into special downloads and installs that that may contain malicious software. Trust in Ads offers guidance on how to avoid these scams in the first in a series of trend reports on bad ads. The site also has a dedicated page at trustinads.org/report with information on how users can easily report any kind of suspicious ad on the group's founding companies' platforms.

CONCLUSION

The Internet is a driver of innovation, communication, and entrepreneurship, which underscores the importance of implementing policies and procedures that protect our users' data. We are committed to developing technology to protect users across the web, contributing research, and facilitating industry initiatives and conversations. We believe that if we all work together to identify threats and stamp them out, we can make the web a safer place for everyone. We look forward to working with this Subcommittee on additional ideas and initiatives to keep users safe online.

Thank you again for your time and consideration.

In: Hidden Hazards of Online Advertising   ISBN: 978-1-63321-458-3
Editor: Lillian Wallace   © 2014 Nova Science Publishers, Inc.

Chapter 4

STATEMENT OF CRAIG D. SPIEZLE, EXECUTIVE DIRECTOR AND PRESIDENT, ONLINE TRUST ALLIANCE. HEARING ON "ONLINE ADVERTISING AND HIDDEN HAZARDS TO CONSUMER SECURITY AND DATA PRIVACY"[*]

Chairman Levin, Ranking Member McCain, and members of the Committee, good morning and thank you for the opportunity to testify before you today.

My name is Craig Spiezle. I am the Executive Director and President of the Online Trust Alliance. OTA is a 501c3 non-profit, with the mission to enhance online trust, empowering users to control their data and privacy, while promoting innovation and the vitality of the internet.

I am testifying to help provide context to the escalating privacy and security threats to consumers resulting from malicious and fraudulent advertising known as malvertising.

As outlined in Exhibit A, malvertising increased over 200% in 2013 to over 209,000 incidents generating over 12.4 billion malicious ad impressions.[1] The impact on consumers is significant. This past January Yahoo experienced an incident resulting in over 300,000 malicious impressions in a single hour.

---

[*] This is an edited, reformatted and augmented version of a statement presented May 15, 2014 before the Senate Homeland Security and Government Affairs Committee, Permanent Subcommittee on Investigations.

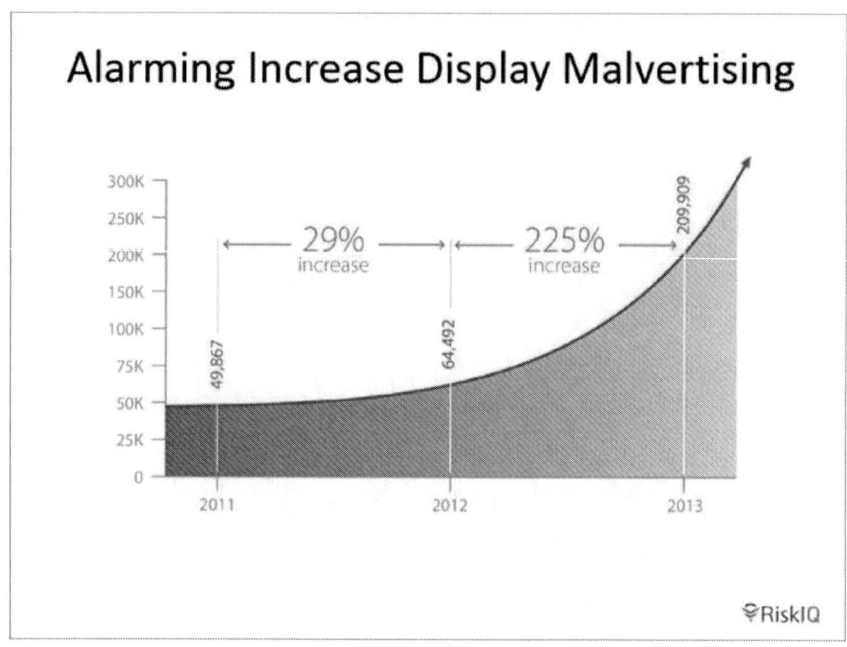

Exhibit A. Malvertising Trends.

Approximately 9% or 27,000 unsuspecting users were compromised. For these consumers, the infection rate was 100%.

This is not an isolated case. Cybercriminals have successfully inserted malicious ads on a range of sites including Google, Microsoft, Facebook, Wall Street Journal, New York Times, Expedia, Major League Baseball, (MLB) and others.[2,3,4]

The threats are significant, with the majority known as "drive by downloads". A drive by is malicious software which runs when a user innocently visits a web site – with no interaction or clicking required.[5] This threat is not new; malvertising was first identified over seven years ago, yet to-date, little progress has been made.

The impact of malvertising ranges from capturing personal information to turning a device into a bot where essentially a cybercriminal can take over that device and use it in many cases to execute a distributed denial-of-service attack (DDoS) against a bank, government agency or other organization. [6] Just as damaging is the deployment of ransomware which encrypts a user's hard drive, demanding payment to be unlocked. Users' personal data, family photos and health records can be destroyed and stolen in seconds.

In the absence of secure online advertising, an impossibly task given today's fragmented advertising ecosystem, the integrity of the internet is at risk. Not unlike pollution in the industrial age, in the absence of regulatory oversight and meaningful self-regulation, these threats continue to grow. The development of coal mining and the use of steam power generated from coal is without doubt the central, binding narrative of the nineteenth century. Jobs were created and profit soared, but the environment soon felt the full impact of industrialization in the form of air and water pollution. Today we are approaching similar cross roads which are undermining the integrity of the internet.

Facing the onslaught of threats, a disturbing trend has emerged with enterprises opting to block all third-party advertising viewed by their employees. This follows users who have been installing ad blockers such as Ad Block Plus and No Script to similarly block all ads.[7, 8] While these tools may help maximize security and privacy, they marginalize the vitality of advertising which supports the sites and services which consumers and business depend on.

HOW DOES MALVERTISING OCCUR?

Since the first banner ads appeared twenty years ago, online advertising and complexity has progressed exponentially.[9] The industry has moved from sites having independent ad sales teams to a complex ecosystem of ad sellers, aggregators and buyers. Stakeholders include advertisers and ad agencies who create ads through a complex arbitrage of ad exchanges, ad networks and demand side platforms (DSP), where ultimately the display ad or ad banner is served through programmatic ad buying. (Exhibit B)[10 11] A typical ad goes through five or six such intermediaries before being served.

The most common tactic to run a malicious ad is the criminal going directly to an ad network, selecting a target audience and paying for an ad campaign. In the absence of reputational checks or threat reporting among the industry, once detected and shut down by one ad network, they simply "water fall" or roll over to other unsuspecting networks to repeat variations of similar exploits.

Other tactics are illustrated in Exhibit C. They include impersonating legitimate advertisers or ad agencies, taking over an employee's user account, actions by rogue employees and the hacking of ad servers compromising existing ads and directly inserting malicious ads.[12]

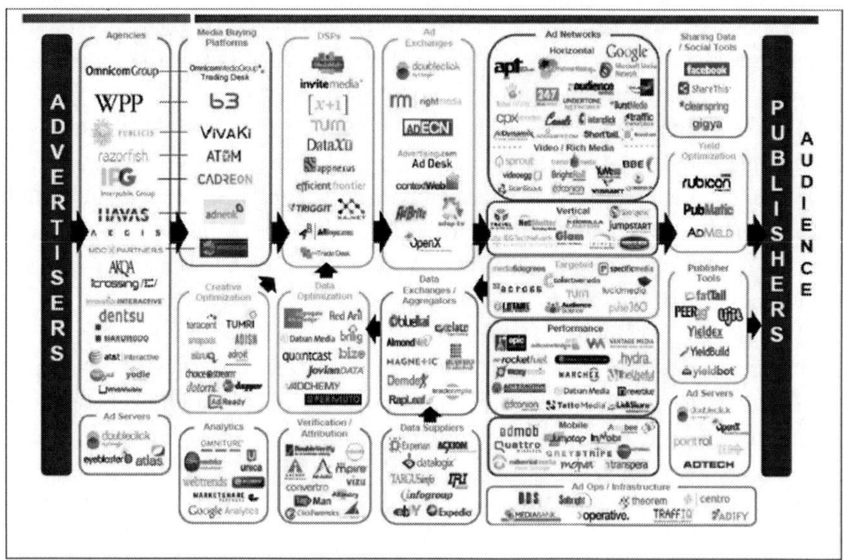

Exhibit B. Interactive Advertising Ecosystem.

Increasingly ads are purchased through an automated process as illustrated in Exhibit D. These systems without human inaction have increased from 38% of total display advertising in 2012 to a forecast of 73% in 2015. While this automation offers significant efficiencies, it lacks robust circuit breakers to detect fraudulent advertisers.[13][14]

The impact of these threats has increased significantly. Criminals are becoming experts in targeting and timing, taking advantage of the powerful tools and data available to internet advertisers. They are data driven marketers with precision to reach vulnerable segments of society or high net worth audiences. This have been enabled to choose the day and time of exploits as well as the type of device they choose to target.

In the absence of policy and traffic quality controls, organized crime has recognized malvertising as the "exploit of choice" offering the ability to be anonymous and remain undetected for days.

INDUSTRY & SELF-REGULATORY EFFORTS

Recognizing the threats of malvertising, in December 2007, DoubleClick, later acquired by Google, established a mailing list which remains today as one of the primary methods of malvertising data sharing. In 2010, OTA established what is now the Advertising and Content Integrity Group, (ACIG), focused on security and fraud prevention best practices. This group of diverse stakeholders leverages a proven model of threat mitigation.[15] This group has since published white papers including a risk evaluation framework and remediation guidelines.[16, 17] These efforts are a small but first step to combat malvertising, reflecting input from leaders including Google, Microsoft, PayPal, Symantec, Twitter and interactive advertisers, web sites and ad agencies.

Last June, StopBadware, a non-profit organization, launched a parallel effort known as the Ads Integrity Alliance. In January 2014, this initiative disbanded due to its members' "desire to refocus their resources on aggressively defending industry practices to policy groups and regulatory bodies".[18]

In the wake of this group's demise, TrustInAds.org was launched last week. According the site, its focus is public policy and raising consumer awareness of the threats and how to report them.[19]

Unfortunately no amount of consumer education can help when users visit trusted web sites that are serving malvertising. Consumers cannot discern good vs malicious ads or how their device was compromised. Focusing on education after the fact is like the auto industry telling accident victims whom to call after an accident from a previously known manufacturing defect, instead of building security features in the cars they sell and profit from.

Other industry efforts have been focused on click fraud, fraudulent activities that attempt to generate revenue by manipulating ad impressions. Click fraud is focused on the monetization and operational issues facing the industry. While efforts to address these issues are underway, do not be confused—click fraud is not related to malvertising's harmful impact on consumers. Click fraud affects websites and advertisers. Malvertising affects consumers.

WHAT IS NEEDED?

OTA proposes a holistic framework addressing five key areas: Prevention, Detection, Notification, Data Sharing and Remediation. Such a framework should be the foundation for an enforceable code of conduct or possible legislation.

1) Prevention – Focused on the development and adoption of controls, systems and safeguards. Networks need to know who their advertisers

are and have methods do identify outliers who may have malicious or fraudulent intent. Stakeholders who fail to adopt reasonable best practices and controls should bear the liability and publishers should reject their ads.

2) Detection – There is no perfect security, but circuit breakers must be in place to help detect abnormal ad behavior. Continuous monitoring is required with 24 /7 incident response teams and abuse desks to both detect and notify stakeholders.

3) Notification & Data Sharing - Escalation paths are needed to share threat intelligence, report abuse and take down threats. Standardized abuse reporting formats and metrics need to be established not unlike those used in the anti-spam and online abuse communities.

4) Remediation – Resources need to be allocated to taking down threats, including addressing any security vulnerabilities in the ecosystem and the user's device that have been compromised.

5) Recovery - Assistance to be provided to users whose devices and accounts have been compromised.

In parallel, operational and technical solutions need to be explored. Ideally we will have solutions where publishers would only allow ads only from networks who vouch for the authenticity of all of the ads they serve, and web browsers will render only such ads that have been signed and verified from trusted sources. It is recognized that such a model would require systemic changes; yet they would increase accountability, protecting the long term vitality of online advertising and most importantly the consumers.

In summary, as a wired society and economy we are increasingly dependent on trustworthy, secure and resilient online services. As observed in every area of our nation's critical infrastructure, we need to recognize that fraudulent businesses, cybercriminals and state sponsored actors will continue to exploit our systems.

For some, malvertising remains a "Black Swan Event", rarely seen but known to exist. For others it is the elephant in the room that no one wants to acknowledge.

Today, companies have little if any incentive to disclose their role or knowledge of a security event, leaving consumers vulnerable and unprotected for potentially months or years, during which time untold amounts of damage can occur. Failure to address these threats suggest the needs for legislation not unlike State data breach laws, requiring mandatory notification, data sharing and remediation to those who have been harmed.

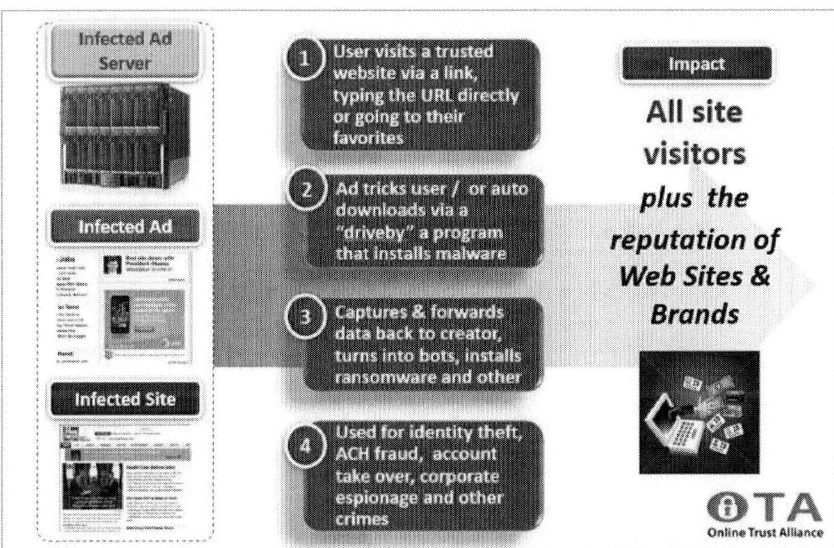

Exhibit C. How Malvertising Works.

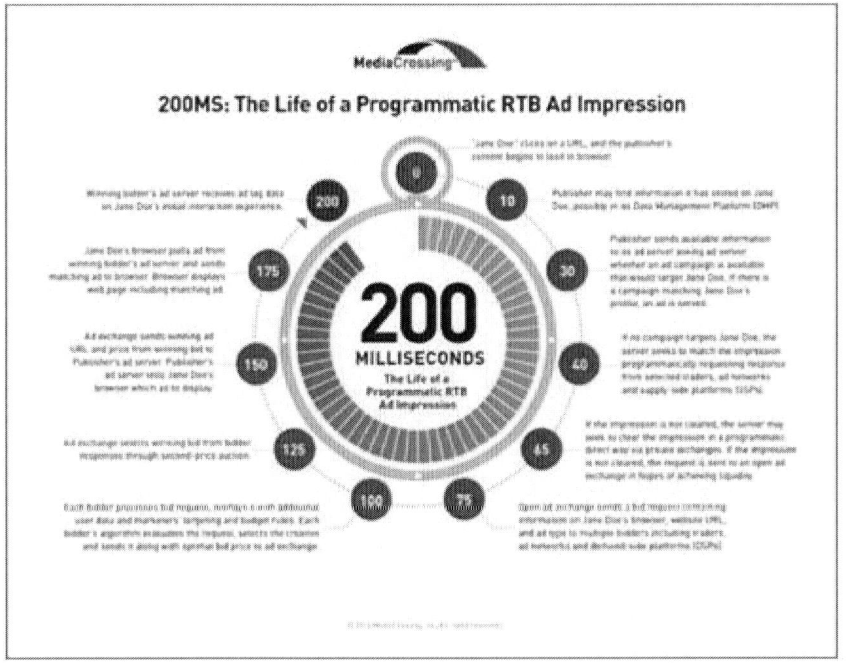

Exhibit D. Programmatic Ad Buying.

As learned from the Target breach, it is the responsibility of a company and its executives to implement safeguards and to heed the warning of the community. The same standards should apply for the ad industry. We must work together, and openly disclose and mediate known vulnerabilities, even at the expense of short-term profits.

It is important to recognize there is no absolute defense against a determined criminal. OTA proposes incentives to companies who adopt best practices and comply with codes of conduct. They should be afforded protection from regulatory oversight as well as frivolous lawsuits. Perceived anti-trust and privacy issues must be resolved to facilitate data sharing to aid in fraud detection and forensics.

Trust is the foundation of every communication we receive, every web site we visit, every transaction we make and every ad we view. Now is the time for action and collaboration, moving from protective silos of information to multi-stakeholder solutions combating cybercrime.

I look forward to your questions. Thank You.

End Notes

[1] OTA data analysis based on incidents reported via data providers including RiskIQ, Zedo, The Media Trust, DoubleClick malvertising group and other sources, factoring in daily site traffic and life of exploit.

[2] http://www.webroot.com/blog/2014/02/14/doubleclick-malvertising-campaign-exposes-long-ru nbeneath-radar-malvertising-infrastructure/

[3] http://blog.trendmicro.com/trendlabs-security-intelligence/malicious-banners-target-expedi aco m-andrhapsodycom/

[4] http://www.scmagazineuk.com/major-league-baseball-website-hit-by-malvertising-that-may-po tentiallyimpact-300000-users/article/246503/

[5] A drive by download is malicious code which executes against a device by simply visiting a site, with no interaction and installs malware. A social engineered exploit is in the form of a pop up or dialog box which attempts to convince a user to take action including downloading a fraudulent update.

[6] http://en.wikipedia.org/wiki/Ransomware(malware)

[7] https://adblockplus.org/en/internet-explorer

[8] http://noscript.net/

[9] http://www.wired.com/2010/10/1027hotwired-banner-ads/

[10] If browser or device cookies are disabled or if a user has enabled anti-tracking mechanisms, they will be served a contextual ad versus one based on the browser habits or profile. If a user turns on "Do Not Track" and the site respects the setting, they would most likely receive contextual based ads.

[11] http://onlineadvertisingecosystem.com/

[12] http://www.tripwire.com/state-of-security/vulnerability-management/analyzing-cve-2013-42 1 1-openxad-server-remote-code-execution-vulnerability/

[13] http://cmsummit.com/behindthebanner/

[14] http://www.adotas.com/2014/05/watch-200-milliseconds-the-life-of-a-programmatic-ad-impre ssion/

[15] https://otalliance.org/resources/botnets/index.html

[16] https://otalliance.org/resources/malvertising.html

[17] https://otalliance.org/docs/Advertising%20Risk%20Evaluation%20Framework.pdf

[18] https://www.stopbadware.org/blog/2014/01/20/stopbadware-steps-down-as-leader-of-the-ads-integrity-alliance

[19] http://trustinads.org/index.html

In: Hidden Hazards of Online Advertising   ISBN: 978-1-63321-458-3
Editor: Lillian Wallace   © 2014 Nova Science Publishers, Inc.

Chapter 5

STATEMENT OF MANEESHA MITHAL, ASSOCIATE DIRECTOR, DIVISION OF PRIVACY AND IDENTITY PROTECTION, FEDERAL TRADE COMMISSION. HEARING ON "ONLINE ADVERTISING AND HIDDEN HAZARDS TO CONSUMER SECURITY AND DATA PRIVACY"[*]

I. INTRODUCTION

Chairman Levin, Ranking Member McCain, and members of the Subcommittee, I am Maneesha Mithal, Associate Director of the Division of Privacy and Identity Protection at the Federal Trade Commission ("FTC" or "Commission").[1] I appreciate the opportunity to present the Commission's testimony on consumer protection issues involving the online advertising industry.

---

[*] This is an edited, reformatted and augmented version of a statement presented May 15, 2014 before the Senate Homeland Security and Government Affairs Committee, Permanent Subcommittee on Investigations.

Online advertising offers many benefits to consumers. It helps support a diverse range of online content and services that otherwise might not be available, or that consumers would otherwise have to pay for – services such as blogging, social networking and instant access to newspapers and information from around the world. It also can be used to tailor offers for products and services most relevant to consumers' interests.

But online behavioral advertising, which entails collecting information about consumers' online activities across websites in order to serve them personalized advertising, can also raise a number of consumer protection concerns. For example, some consumers may be uncomfortable with the privacy implications of being tracked across the websites they visit, or may be unaware that this practice is even occurring. And, without adequate safeguards in place, consumer tracking data may fall into the wrong hands or be used for adverse unanticipated purposes, including transmission to other third parties. These concerns are exacerbated when the tracking involves sensitive information about, for example, children, health, or a consumer's finances. Finally, online advertising can be used to deliver spyware and other malware to cause a host of problems to consumers' computers.

As the nation's consumer protection agency, the FTC is committed to protecting consumers in the online marketplace. The Commission is primarily a civil law enforcement agency, and its main operative statute is Section 5 of the FTC Act, which prohibits unfair or deceptive acts or practices in or affecting commerce.[2] A company acts deceptively if it makes materially misleading statements or omissions.[3] A company engages in unfair acts or practices if its practices cause or are likely to cause substantial injury to consumers that is neither reasonably avoidable by consumers nor outweighed by countervailing benefits to consumers or to competition.[4] The Commission uses its enforcement authority under Section 5 to take action against online advertising companies and others engaged in unfair or deceptive practices. It also educates consumers and businesses about the online environment and encourages industry self-regulation.

This testimony will discuss the Commission's work to address three consumer protection issues affecting the online advertising industry: privacy, malware, and data security. It will then provide some recommendations for next steps in this area.

II. CONSUMER PROTECTION ISSUES AFFECTING THE ONLINE ADVERTISING INDUSTRY

A. Privacy

Since online privacy first emerged as a significant issue in the mid-1990s, it has been one of the Commission's highest consumer protection priorities. The Commission has worked to address privacy issues in the online marketplace, particularly those raised by online advertising networks, through consumer and business education, law enforcement, and policy initiatives.

Throughout the last decade, the FTC has examined the privacy implications of online behavioral advertising through a number of workshops and reports.[5] In March of 2012, the Commission released its Privacy Report, which set forth best practices for businesses – including the online advertising industry – to protect consumer privacy while ensuring that companies can continue to innovate.[6] The report called on companies to provide simpler and more streamlined choices to consumers about their data, through a robust universal choice mechanism for online behavioral advertising.[7]

The Commission has also engaged in a number of privacy enforcement actions involving the online advertising industry. For example, in its first online behavioral advertising case, the Commission alleged that online advertising network Chitika violated the FTC Act's prohibition on deceptive practices when it offered consumers the ability to opt out of the collection of information to be used for targeted advertising – without telling them that the opt-out lasted only ten days.[8] The Commission's order prohibits Chitika from making future privacy misrepresentations. It also requires Chitika to provide consumers with an effective opt-out mechanism, link to this opt-out mechanism in its advertisements, and provide a notice on its website for consumers who may have opted out when Chitika's opt-out mechanism was ineffective. Finally, the order required Chitika to destroy any data that can be associated with a consumer that it collected during the time its opt-out mechanism was ineffective.

Online ad network ScanScout also settled FTC charges that it deceptively claimed that consumers could opt out of receiving targeted ads by changing their computer's web browser settings to block cookies.[9] In fact, ScanScout used Flash cookies, which browser settings could not block. Under the terms of the order, ScanScout is prohibited from misrepresenting the company's data collection practices and consumers' ability to control collection of their data. It also requires ScanScout to improve disclosure of its data collection practices and to provide a user-friendly mechanism that allows consumers to opt out of being tracked.

Epic Marketplace, an online ad network, settled charges that it used "history sniffing" to secretly and illegally gather data from millions of consumers about their interest in sensitive medical and financial issues ranging from fertility and incontinence to debt relief and personal bankruptcy.[10] As explained in the complaint, Epic Marketplace is a large advertising network with a presence on 45,000 websites. Consumers who visited any of the network's sites received a cookie, which stored information about their online practices including sites they visited and the ads they viewed. The cookies allowed Epic to serve consumers behaviorally targeted ads. Despite claims that it would collect information only about consumers' visits to sites in its network, Epic was employing "history-sniffing" technology that allowed it to collect data about sites outside its network that consumers had visited, including sites relating to personal health conditions and finances. The FTC alleged that the history sniffing was deceptive and allowed Epic to determine whether a consumer had visited any of more than 54,000 domains, including pages relating to fertility issues, impotence, menopause, incontinence, disability insurance, credit repair, debt relief, and personal bankruptcy. The order imposed similar relief to the other cases in this area.

Finally, in 2012 Google agreed to pay a record $22.5 million civil penalty to settle charges that it misrepresented to Safari browser users that it would not place tracking cookies or serve targeted ads to them, [11] violating an earlier privacy order with the Commission.[12] In its complaint, the FTC alleged that for several months, Google placed a certain advertising tracking cookie on the computers of Safari users who visited sites within Google's DoubleClick advertising network, although Google had previously told these users they would automatically be opted out of such tracking, as a result of the Safari browser default settings. Despite these promises, the FTC alleged that Google placed advertising tracking cookies on consumers' computers, in many cases by circumventing the Safari browser's default cookie-blocking setting.[13] According to the complaint, Google's misrepresentations violated an earlier FTC order, which barred Google from – among other things – misrepresenting the extent to which consumers can exercise control over the collection of their information.

B. Spyware and Other Malware

Spyware and other malware can cause substantial harm to consumers and to the Internet as a medium of communication and commerce. When downloaded without authorization, including through online ads, spyware and other malware can cause a range of problems for computer users, from nuisance adware that delivers pop-up ads, to software that causes sluggish computer performance, to keystroke loggers that capture sensitive information.

The Commission has sought to address concerns about spyware and other malware through law enforcement and consumer education. Since 2004, the Commission has initiated a number of malware-related law enforcement actions, which reaffirm three key principles. The first is that a consumer's computer belongs to him or her, not to the software distributor, and it must be the consumer's choice whether or not to install software. This principle reflects the basic common-sense notion that Internet businesses are not free to help themselves to the resources of a consumer's computer. For example, in *FTC v. Seismic Entertainment Inc.,*[14] and *FTC v. Enternet Media, Inc.,*[15] the Commission alleged that the defendants unfairly downloaded spyware to users' computers without the users' knowledge, in violation of Section 5 of the FTC Act. And, in its case against CyberSpy Software LLC, the FTC alleged that the defendants unfairly sold keylogging software to others that could be downloaded to users' computers without their knowledge or consent.[16]

The second principle is that buried disclosures of material information necessary to correct an otherwise misleading impression are not sufficient in connection with software downloads, just as they have never been sufficient in more traditional areas of commerce. Specifically, burying material information in an End User License Agreement will not shield a malware purveyor from Section 5 liability. This principle was illustrated in *FTC v. Odysseus Marketing, Inc.*[17] and *Advertising.com, Inc.*[18] In these two cases, the Commission alleged (among other violations) that the companies failed to disclose adequately that the free software they were offering was bundled with harmful software programs.

The third principle is that, if a distributor puts a program on a computer that the consumer does not want, the consumer should be able to uninstall or disable it. This principle is underscored by the FTC's cases against Zango, Inc.[19] and DirectRevenue LLC.[20] These companies allegedly provided advertising programs, or adware, that monitored consumers' Internet use and displayed frequent, targeted pop-up ads – over 6.9 billion pop-ups by Zango alone. According to the Commission's complaints, the companies deliberately made these adware programs difficult for consumers to identify, locate, and remove from their computers, thus thwarting consumer efforts to end the intrusive pop-ups. Among other relief, the consent orders require Zango and DirectRevenue to provide a readily identifiable means to uninstall any adware that is installed in the future, as well as to disgorge $3 million and $1.5 million, respectively.

In addition to engaging in law enforcement, the FTC has made consumer education on malware issues a priority. The Commission sponsors OnGuard Online, a website designed to educate consumers about basic computer security. [21] OnGuard Online and its Spanish-language counterpart, Alerta en Línea,[22] average more than 2.2 million unique visits per year. The comprehensive web site has general information on online safety, as well as sections with detailed information on a range of topics, including spyware. And, the FTC also has created a number of articles, videos, and games available to consumers on both its website[23] and OnGuard Online to describe the threats associated with spyware and malware as well as provide consumers with information about how to avoid and detect such malicious software.

C. Data Security

While taking action against the purveyors of malware is important, it is also critical to ensure that companies are taking reasonable steps to ensure that they are not inadvertently enabling third parties to place malware on consumers' computers. To this end, online advertising networks should maintain reasonable safeguards to ensure that they are not displaying advertisements containing malware that can slow down consumers' computers, expose them to unwanted content such as pop-up ads, and gain unauthorized access to their personal information.

The Commission has undertaken substantial efforts for over a decade to promote strong data security practices in the private sector in order to prevent hackers and purveyors of malware from harming consumers. In addition to enforcing Section 5 of the FTC Act, discussed above, the Commission enforces several specific statutes and rules that impose obligations upon businesses to protect consumer data. The Commission's Safeguards Rule, which implements the Gramm-Leach-Bliley Act, for example, provides data security requirements for non-bank financial institutions.[24] The Fair Credit Reporting Act requires consumer reporting agencies to use reasonable procedures to ensure that the entities to which they disclose sensitive consumer information have a permissible purpose for receiving that information,[25] and imposes safe disposal obligations on entities that maintain consumer report information.[26] The Children's Online Privacy Protection Act requires reasonable security for children's information collected online.[27] Reasonableness is the foundation of the data security provisions of each of these laws.

The FTC conducts its data security investigations to determine whether a company's data security measures are reasonable and appropriate in light of the sensitivity and volume of consumer information it holds, the size and complexity of its data operations, and the cost of available tools to improve security and reduce vulnerabilities. The Commission's 53 settlements with businesses that it charged with failing to provide reasonable protections for consumers' personal information have halted harmful data security practices; required companies to provide strong protections for consumer data; and raised awareness about the risks to data, the need for reasonable and appropriate security, and the types of security failures that raise concerns.[28]

In its most recent data security case, the FTC announced a settlement with Snapchat, Inc., a company that markets a popular mobile application ("app") that allows consumers to send and receive photo and video messages known as "snaps."[29] According to the complaint, Snapchat misrepresented that its app provided a private, short-lived messaging service, claiming that once the consumer-set timer for a viewed snap expired, the snap "disappears forever." Snapchat's app has a "Find Friends" feature that allows consumers to find and communicate with friends who use the Snapchat service. However, unbeknownst to users, the Find Friends feature collected the names and phone numbers of all contacts in a user's mobile device address book and had major security flaws. The complaint alleges that Snapchat violated Section 5 by misrepresenting the disappearing nature of messages sent through its app and the amount of personal information that its app would collect for the Find Friends feature.

The complaint also charges that despite its claims regarding reasonable security, Snapchat failed to adequately secure the Find Friends feature, which led to significant misuse and unauthorized disclosure of consumers' personal information. For example, the complaint alleges that numerous consumers complained that they had sent snaps to someone who impersonated a friend. In fact, because Snapchat failed to verify users' phone numbers during registration, these consumers were actually sending their personal snaps to complete strangers who had registered with phone numbers that did not belong to them. Moreover, in December 2013, Snapchat's failures allowed attackers to compile a database of 4.6 million Snapchat usernames and phone numbers, which could have subjected consumers to costly spam, phishing and other unsolicited communications.

The FTC also recently entered into settlements with Credit Karma, Inc.[30] and Fandango, LLC.[31] to resolve allegations that the companies misrepresented the security of their mobile apps.

Credit Karma's mobile app allows consumers to monitor and access their credit scores, credit reports, and other credit report and financial data, and has been downloaded over one million times. Fandango's mobile app allows consumers to purchase movie tickets and has over 18.5 million downloads. According to the complaints, despite claims that the companies provided reasonable security to consumers' data, Credit Karma and Fandango did not securely transmit consumers' sensitive personal information through their mobile apps. In particular, the apps failed to authenticate and secure the connections used to transmit this data, and left consumers' information vulnerable to exposure – including Social Security numbers, birthdates, and credit report information in the Credit Karma app, and credit card information in the Fandango app. The Commission's settlements prohibit Credit Karma and Fandango from making misrepresentations about privacy and security, and require the companies to implement comprehensive information security programs and undergo independent audits for the next 20 years.

Finally, the FTC announced a case against TRENDnet, Inc., which involved a video camera designed to allow consumers to monitor their homes remotely.[32] The complaint alleges that TRENDnet marketed its SecurView cameras for purposes ranging from home security to baby monitoring. Although TRENDnet claimed that the cameras were "secure," they had faulty software that left them open to online viewing, and in some instances listening, by anyone with a camera's Internet address. This resulted in hackers posting 700 consumers' live video feeds on the Internet. Under the FTC settlement, TRENDnet must maintain a comprehensive security program, obtain outside audits, notify consumers about the security issues and the availability of software updates to correct them, and provide affected customers with free technical support for the next two years.

In each of its 53 data security cases, the Commission has examined a company's practices as a whole and challenged alleged data security failures that were multiple and systemic. Through these settlements, the Commission has made clear that reasonable and appropriate security is a continuous process of assessing and addressing risks; that there is no one-size-fits-all data security program; that the Commission does not require perfect security; and that the mere fact that a breach occurred does not mean that a company has violated the law. These principles apply equally to advertising networks. Just because malware has been installed does not mean that the advertising network has violated Section 5. Rather, the Commission would look to whether the advertising network took reasonable steps to prevent third parties from using online ads to deliver malware.

III. RECOMMENDATIONS FOR NEXT STEPS

The Commission shares this Committee's concerns about the use of online advertisements to deliver malware onto consumers' computers, which implicates each of the areas discussed in this testimony – consumer privacy, malware, and data security. We encourage several additional steps to protect consumers in this area.

The first is more widespread consumer education about how consumers can protect their computers against malware. The FTC materials discussed in this testimony are available at www.OnguardOnline.gov and www.ftc.gov. We encourage businesses, advocacy organizations, and other government agencies at the state, local, and federal levels to use these materials and tailor them to their particular constituencies and concerns.

The second is continued industry self-regulation to ensure that ad networks are taking reasonable steps to prevent the use of their systems to display malicious ads to consumers. Just last week, Facebook, Google and Twitter publicly unveiled TrustInAds.org, a new organization aimed at protecting people from malicious online advertisements.[33] The companies report that they will bring awareness to consumers about online ad-related scams and deceptive activities, collaborate to identify trends, and share their knowledge with policymakers and consumer advocates. In addition, the Online Trust Alliance has published guidelines for companies in this area, along with a risk evaluation tool.[34] The Commission applauds these groups for taking steps to address this issue.

Finally, the Commission continues to reiterate its longstanding, bipartisan call for enactment of a strong federal data security and breach notification law. Reasonable and appropriate security practices are critical to preventing data breaches and protecting consumers from identity theft and other harm. Despite the threats posed by data breaches, many companies continue to underinvest in data security. For example, the Commission's settlements have shown that some companies fail to take even the most basic security precautions, such as updating antivirus software or requiring network administrators to use strong passwords. With reports of data breaches on the rise, and with a significant number of Americans suffering from identity theft, having a strong and uniform national data security requirement would reinforce the requirement under the FTC Act that companies must implement reasonable measures to ensure that consumers' personal information is protected. Although most states have breach notification laws in place, having a strong and consistent national breach notification requirement would simplify compliance by businesses while ensuring that all consumers are protected.

Among other things, such legislation would supplement the Commission's existing data security authority by authorizing the Commission to seek civil penalties in appropriate circumstances against companies that do not reasonably protect consumers' data. Providing the Commission with authority to seek civil penalties in these cases would help deter unlawful conduct, including using malware to gain access to consumers' personal information – such as through keystroke loggers. Such legislation could provide the Commission with an important consumer protection tool.

CONCLUSION

Thank you for the opportunity to provide the Commission's testimony on consumer protection issues involving the online advertising industry. We look forward to continuing to work with the Subcommittee and Congress on this important issue.

End Notes

[1] This written statement presents the views of the Federal Trade Commission. My oral statements and responses to questions are my own and do not necessarily reflect the views of the Commission or of any Commissioner.

[2] 15 U.S.C. § 45(a). The Commission also enforces numerous specific statutes.

[3] See Federal Trade Commission Policy Statement on Deception, appended to Cliffdale Assocs., Inc., 103 F.T.C. 110, 174 (1984).

[4] See 15 U.S.C. § 45(n); Federal Trade Commission Policy Statement on Unfairness, appended to Int'l Harvester Co., 104 F.T.C. 949, 1070 (1984) ("FTC Unfairness Statement").

[5] See, e.g., FTC Press Release, Staff Proposes Online Behavioral Advertising Policy Principles (Dec. 20, 2007), available at http://www.ftc.gov/news-events/press-releases/2007/12/ftc-staff-proposes-onlinebehavioral-advertising-privacy; FTC Town Hall, Ehavioral Advertising: Tracking, Targeting, & Technology (Nov. 1-2, 2007), available at http://www.

ftc.gov/news-events/eventscalendar/2007/11/ehavioral-advertising-tracking-targeting-technology; FTC Workshop, Protecting Consumers in the Next Tech-Ade (Nov. 6-9, 2006), available at http://www.ftc.gov/news-events/eventscalendar/2006/11/protecting-consumers-next-tech-ade; FTC Staff Report, Self-Regulatory Principles for Online Behavioral Advertising (Feb. 2009), available at http://www.ftc.gov/sites/default/files/ documents/reports/federal-trade-commission-staff-report-selfregulatory-principles-online-behavioral-advertising/p085400behavadreport.pdf.

[6] FTC Report, Protecting Consumers in an Era of Rapid Change: Recommendations for Businesses and Policymakers (Mar. 2012) ("Privacy Report"), available at http://www.ftc.gov/sites/default/files/documents/reports/federal-trade-commission-report-protecting-consumer-privacy-era-rapid-change-recommendations/120326privacyreport.pdf. Commissioner Ohlhausen and Commissioner Wright were not members of the Commission at that time and thus did not participate in the vote on the report.

[7] In the Privacy Report, the Commission articulated five essential elements of a robust do-not-track mechanism: universal, persistent, easy to find and use, effective, and that the mechanism provide control over the collection of information, not just the delivery of targeted ads. Id. at 53.

[8] Chitika, Inc., No. C-4324 (F.T.C. June 7, 2011) (consent order), available at http://www.ftc.gov/enforcement/cases-proceedings/1023087/chitika-inc-matter.

[9] ScanScout, Inc., No. C-4344 (F.T.C. Dec. 14, 2011) (consent order), available at http://www.ftc.gov/enforcement/cases-proceedings/102-3185/scanscout-inc-matter.

[10] Epic Marketplace, Inc., No. C-4389 (F.T.C. Mar. 13, 2013), available at http://www.ftc.gov/enforcement/cases-proceedings/112-3182/epic-marketplace-inc.

[11] United States v. Google, Inc., No. 512-cv-04177-HRL (N.D. Cal. Nov. 16, 2012), available at http://www.ftc.gov/enforcement/cases-proceedings/google-inc.

[12] Google, Inc., No. C-4336 (F.T.C. Oct. 13, 2011), available at http://www.ftc.gov/enforcement/casesproceedings/102-3136/google-inc-matter.

[13] Google used an exception to the browser's default setting to place a temporary cookie from the DoubleClick domain. Because of the particular operation of the Safari browser, that initial temporary cookie opened the door to all cookies from the DoubleClick domain, including the Google advertising tracking cookie that Google had represented would be blocked from Safari browsers.

[14] FTC v. Seismic Entertainment Productions, Inc., et al., No. 04-377-JD (D.N.H. 2006), available at http://www.ftc.gov/enforcement/cases-proceedings/042-3142-x05-0013/seismic-entertainmentproductions-inc-et-al.

[15] FTC v. Enternet Media Inc. et al., No. CV 05-777 CAS (C.D. Cal. 2006), available at http://www.ftc.gov/enforcement/cases-proceedings/052-3135-x06-0003/enternet-media-inc-conspy-coinc-et-al.

[16] FTC v. CyberSpy Software, LLC, No. 6:08-cv-1872-ORL-31GJK (M.D. Fla. 2010), available at http://www.ftc.gov/enforcement/cases-proceedings/082-3160/cyberspy-software-llc-trace r spence.

[17] FTC v. Odysseus Marketing, Inc., No. 05-CV-330 (D.N.H. 2006), available at http:// www. ftc.gov/enforcement/cases-proceedings/042-3205-x050069/odysseus-marketing-inc-walter-rines.

[18] Advertising.com, Inc., No. C-4147 (F.T.C. Sept. 12, 2005) (consent order), available at http://www.ftc.gov/enforcement/cases-proceedings/042-3196/advertisingcom-inc-et-al-matter.

[19] Zango, Inc. f/k/a 180 Solutions, Inc., No. C-4186 (F.T.C. Mar. 7, 2007) (consent order), available at http://www.ftc.gov/enforcement/cases-proceedings/052-3130/zango-inc-fka-180solutions-inc-et-almatter.

[20] DirectRevenue LLC, No. C-4194 (F.T.C. June 26, 2007) (consent order), available at http://www.ftc.gov/enforcement/cases-proceedings/052-3131/directrevenue-llc-et-al.

[21] See http://www.onguardonline.gov.

[22] See http://www.alertaenlinea.gov.

[23] See generally http://www.consumer.ftc.gov.

[24] 16 C.F.R. Part 314, implementing 15 U.S.C. § 6801(b).

[25] 15 U.S.C. § 1681e.

[26] Id. at § 1681w. The FTC's implementing rule is at 16 C.F.R. Part 682.

[27] 15 U.S.C. §§ 6501-6506; see also 16 C.F.R. Part 312 ("COPPA Rule").

[28] See Commission Statement Marking the FTC's 50th Data Security Settlement, Jan. 31, 2014, available at http://www.ftc.gov/system/files/documents/cases/140131gmrstatement.pdf.

[29] Snapchat, Inc., No. 132-3078 (F.T.C. May 8, 2014) (proposed consent agreement), available at http://www.ftc.gov/enforcement/cases-proceedings/132-3078/snapchat-inc-matter.

[30] Credit Karma, Inc., No. 132-3091 (F.T.C. Mar. 28, 2014) (proposed consent agreement), available at http://www.ftc.gov/enforcement/cases-proceedings/132-3091/credit-karma-inc.

[31] Fandango, LLC, No. 132-3089 (F.T.C. Mar. 28, 2014) (proposed consent agreement), available at http://www.ftc.gov/enforcement/cases-proceedings/132-3089/fandango-llc.

[32] TRENDnet, Inc., No. C-4426(F.T.C. Jan. 16, 2014) (consent order), available at http://www.ftc.gov/enforcement/cases-proceedings/122-3090/trendnet-inc-matter.

[33] See generally http://www.trustinads.org.

[34] See generally Online Trust Alliance, Advertising & Content Publishing Supply Chain Integrity (Apr. 1, 2014), available at https://otalliance.org/resources/malvertising.html.

In: Hidden Hazards of Online Advertising
Editor: Lillian Wallace

ISBN: 978-1-63321-458-3
© 2014 Nova Science Publishers, Inc.

Chapter 6

TESTIMONY OF LUIGI MASTRIA, EXECUTIVE DIRECTOR, DIGITAL ADVERTISING ALLIANCE. HEARING ON "ONLINE ADVERTISING AND HIDDEN HAZARDS TO CONSUMER SECURITY AND DATA PRIVACY"[*]

Chairman Levin, Ranking Member McCain, and Members of the Subcommittee, good morning and thank you for the opportunity to speak at this important hearing.

My name is Lou Mastria. I am Executive Director of the Digital Advertising Alliance ("DAA") and I am pleased to report to the Committee on the substantial progress of our Self-Regulatory Program that is providing consumers transparency and choice.

The DAA is a non-profit organization led by the leading advertising and marketing trade associations including the Association of National Advertisers ("ANA"), the American Association of Advertising Agencies ("4As"), the Direct Marketing Association ("DMA"), the Interactive Advertising Bureau ("IAB"), the American Advertising Federation ("AAF"), and the Network Advertising Initiative ("NAI"), in consultation with the Council of Better Business Bureaus ("CBBB"). These organizations came together in 2008 to

---

[*] This is an edited, reformatted and augmented version of testimony presented May 15, 2014 before the Senate Homeland Security and Government Affairs Committee, Permanent Subcommittee on Investigations.

start developing the Self-Regulatory Principles for Online Behavioral Advertising, which were extended in 2011 beyond advertising to cover the collection and use of Multi-Site Data across non-Affiliate sites over time, and then again extended in July 2013 to provide guidance for data collection in mobile environments. The DAA was formed to administer and promote these responsible and comprehensive Self-Regulatory Principles for online data collection and use.

The DAA is a model example of how interested stakeholders can collaborate to provide flexible, market-driven solutions to complex privacy issues. In my testimony, I will describe the benefits of online advertising and how the industry through the DAA provides consumer-friendly privacy standards in a way that also ensures the continued vibrancy of the Internet and our nation's place as the global leader in the data-driven economy.

I. BENEFITS OF ONLINE ADVERTISING

The Internet is a tremendous engine of economic growth. It has become the focus and a symbol of the United States' famed innovation, ingenuity, inventiveness, and entrepreneurial spirit, as well as the venture funding that follows. Simply put: the Internet economy and the interactive advertising industry create jobs. A 2012 study found that the Internet economy supports the employment of more than five million Americans, contributing an estimated $530 billion, or approximately 3%, to our country's GDP.[1] There is Internet employment in every single state.[2] Another recent study, commissioned by DMA's Data-Driven Marketing Institute ("DDMI") and conducted independently by Professors John Deighton of Harvard Business School and Peter Johnson of Columbia University, and entitled "The Value of Data: Consequences for Insight, Innovation & Efficiency in the U.S. Economy" ("Value of Data"), quantifies the value data has to our economy. The Value of Data study found that the Data-Driven Market Economy ("DDME") added $156 billion in revenue to the U.S. economy and fueled more than 675,000 jobs in 2012 alone. The study also found that an additional 1,038,000 jobs owe part of their existence to these DDME jobs. The study estimated that 70% of the value of the DDME – $110 billion in revenue and 475,000 jobs nationwide – depends on the ability of firms to share data across the DDME.

Advertising fuels this powerful Internet economic engine. The support provided by online advertising is substantial. In 2013, Internet advertising revenues reached a new high of \$43 billion, an impressive 17% higher than 2012's full-year number.[3]

Because of advertising, consumers can access a wealth of online resources at low or no cost. Revenue from online advertising enables e-commerce and subsidizes the cost of content and services that consumers value, such as online newspapers, blogs, social networking sites, mobile applications, email, and phone services. These advertising-supported resources have transformed our daily lives.

Interest-based advertising is an essential form of online advertising. Interest-based advertising is delivered based on consumer preferences or interests as inferred from data about online activities. Consumers are likely to find interest-based advertisements more relevant to them, and advertisers are more likely to attract consumers that want their products and services.

Interest-based advertising is especially vital for small businesses because it is efficient. Smaller advertisers can stretch their marketing budgets to reach consumers who may be interested in their offerings. Smaller website publishers that cannot afford to employ sales personnel to sell their advertising space, and may be less attractive to large brand-name advertising campaigns, can increase their revenue by featuring advertising that is more relevant to their users. In turn, advertising-supported resources help other small businesses to grow. Small businesses can use free or low-cost online tools, such as travel booking, long-distance calling, and networking services, to help them run their companies.

II. THE DAA

As the DAA was convened, its goal was to provide greater transparency and control to consumers with respect to their Web viewing data while preserving these incredible benefits to consumers and our economy. Since 2008, the DAA has worked with a broad set of stakeholders with significant input from businesses, consumers, and policy makers to develop a program governing the responsible collection and use of Web viewing data. This work led to the development of the groundbreaking *Self-Regulatory Principles for Online Behavioral Advertising* ("Principles"), released in 2009.

The DAA approach provides consumers choice with respect to collection and use of their Internet viewing data while preserving the ability of companies to responsibly deliver services and continue innovating. This approach allows consumers to enjoy the incredibly diverse range of Web sites by preserving the responsible data flows that support these offerings and that fuel our nation's economy.

The DAA Principles apply broadly to the diverse set of actors that work interdependently to deliver relevant advertising intended to enrich the consumer digital experience, and to foster consumer-friendly privacy standards that are to be applied throughout the ecosystem. The Principles were developed over a year-long period in which broad consensus was reached among the key constituencies of the Internet community. These Principles call for (1) enhanced notice outside of the privacy policy so that consumers can be made aware of the companies they interact with while using the Internet, (2) the provision of choice mechanisms, (3) education, and (4) strong enforcement mechanisms. Together, these Principles increase consumers' trust and confidence in how information is gathered online and in mobile environments and how it is used to deliver advertisements based on their interests.

A. Consumer Disclosure through the DAA Icon ▷

The DAA program has developed a universal icon to give consumers transparency and control with respect to interest-based ads. The icon provides consumers with notice that information about their online interests is being gathered to customize the Web ads they see.

Clicking the icon also takes consumers to a centralized choice tool that enables consumers to opt out of this type of advertising by participating companies.

The icon is served globally more than *one trillion times each month* on or next to Internet display ads, websites, and other digital properties and tools covered by the program. This achievement represents an unprecedented level of industry cooperation and adoption.

B. Consumer Control

At DAA's *www.aboutads.info* website and accessible from the companion *www.YourAdChoices.com* website, the DAA program makes available a choice mechanism that unites the opt-out mechanisms provided by more than 115 different third-party advertisers participating in the program. The choice mechanism offers consumers a "one-click" option to request opt outs from all participants or allows a user to make choices about specific companies.

Consumers are directed to aboutads.info not only from DAA icon-based disclosures on or around ads, but from other forms of website disclosure. In 2012, the DAA also introduced a suite of browser plug-ins to help ensure the persistency of these choices.

Since program launch, there have been more than 30 million unique visitors to the DAA program Web sites. *Over three million unique users* have exercised choice using the integrated opt-out mechanism provided at AboutAds.info. Many users visit DAA program Web sites, learn about their choices, and ultimately choose not to opt out. This shows that once consumers understand how online advertising works, many prefer to receive relevant ads over irrelevant ads. Research supports this proposition. A recent poll of U.S. consumers shows that 68 percent of Americans prefer to get at least some Internet ads directed at their interests and 40 percent of Americans prefer to get *all* their ads directed to their interests.[4]

C. Consumer Education

The DAA is also committed to consumer education. The DAA launched a dedicated educational site at *www.YourAdChoices.com* to provide easy-to-understand messaging and informative videos explaining the choices available to consumers, the meaning of the DAA icon, and the benefits they derive from online advertising. Companies participating in the DAA program have donated voluntarily more than four billion impressions to support an educational campaign for *www.YourAdChoices.com*. More than *15 million unique users* have visited this site. This site also provides access to the DAA's user choice mechanism. The combination of the educational campaign and the ubiquitous availability of the DAA icon have significantly increased consumer usage of the DAA program tools.

D. Accountability

For the past 40 years, the advertising industry has distinguished itself through its self-regulatory systems for independent oversight of compliance and public reporting of enforcement actions. In keeping with this tradition, a key feature of the DAA Self-Regulatory Program is accountability. All of the DAA's Self-Regulatory Principles are backed by the robust enforcement programs administered by the Council of Better Business Bureaus ("CBBB") under the policy guidance of the Advertising Self-Regulatory Council (ASRC), and by the DMA under its Guidelines for Ethical Business Practice. In addition to the oversight provided by the CBBB and DMA compliance programs, the NAI also has a strong compliance program. The NAI's compliance program, like the CBBB and DMA programs, helps members to comply with their self-regulatory obligations, and to hold them accountable.[5] A more detailed description of how these programs work is included in Appendix I.

E. Application of Self-Regulatory Principles to Data Collected on Mobile Devices

The DAA Self-Regulatory Program has adapted over time and we expect this evolution to continue with changes in the marketplace driven by technological advancements and evolving consumer preferences. In July 2013, the DAA issued new implementation guidance addressing operation across a variety of channels including mobile. The guidance explains how the Self-Regulatory Principles apply to certain data practices that may occur on mobile or other devices.

Stakeholders representing all major elements of the mobile ecosystem participated in the development of this guidance. The guidance describes how the Self-Regulatory Principles apply to the mobile web environment and to the application environment, which DAA calls "Cross-App" data – data collected from a device across non-Affiliated applications over time. The DAA has now turned its work with DAA stakeholders to develop and implement a companion choice mechanism for Cross-App Data. This new tool will offer consumers an unprecedented level of control over data collection across applications on a device.

The successful approach taken by the DAA led to an event in February 2012 at the White House where the Chairman of the Federal Trade Commission ("FTC"), the Secretary of Commerce, and White House officials publicly praised the DAA's cross-industry initiative. The White House recognized our Self-Regulatory Program as "an example of the value of industry leadership as a critical part of privacy protection going forward." Since the White House event, the DAA's further work in releasing the Self-Regulatory Principles for Multi-Site Data (November 2011) and guidance on the Application of Self-Regulatory Principles to the Mobile Environment (July 2013) has garnered additional praise, including from FTC Commissioner

Ohlhausen who has stated that the DAA "is one of the great success stories in the [privacy] space."

CONCLUSION

The DAA has championed consumer control that both accommodates consumers' privacy expectations and supports the ability of companies to responsibly deliver services desired by consumers and continue innovating. We appreciate the opportunity to be here today. We believe our successful model can continue to effectively evolve in the privacy area and can also be replicated in other areas.

I am pleased to answer any questions that you may have.

APPENDIX I: ACCOUNTABILITY PROGRAMS

The CBBB Accountability Program builds on the successful track records of the other ASRC programs: the National Advertising Division, operating since 1971; the Children's Advertising Review Unit, operating since 1974; and the Electronic Retailing Self-Regulation Program, operating since 2004. These programs feature independent monitoring; public reporting of decisions; and referral to government agencies, often to the FTC, of any uncorrected non-compliance. They have extremely high voluntary compliance rates. In fact, over 90 percent of companies voluntarily adopt the recommendations of these programs. Those companies that fail to comply or refuse to participate in the self-regulatory enforcement process are referred publicly to the appropriate government agency for further review.

The CBBB administers its Interest-Based Advertising Accountability Program under the ASRC self-regulatory policy guidance and procedures. Because of the highly complex, technical and interdependent nature of interest-based advertising, the Accountability Program receives a weekly privacy dashboard report based on independent data about more than 250 companies' compliance with various requirements of the Principles. The Accountability Program's technical staff analyzes these data and independently performs further research to determine whether there may be a violation of the Principles warranting formal inquiry. Like other ASRC programs administered by the CBBB, the CBBB Accountability Program also finds potential cases through its own staff monitoring and investigation, by analysis of consumer complaints and reviews of news stories and technical reports from academics and advocacy groups. Where there is a potential compliance issue, the CBBB initiates formal inquiries and works to ensure the company understands the Principles and voluntarily implements the requirements of the Principles. At the end of the process, the CBBB Accountability Program issues a public decision, which details the nature of the inquiry, the Accountability Program's conclusions, any recommendations for correction, and includes a statement from the company in question regarding its implementation of the recommendations. A press release is also issued.

The CBBB's Accountability Program has brought 33 cases since November 2011. The CBBB Accountability Program has focused its inquiries on the key concepts of transparency and choice under the DAA's Self-Regulatory Principles. In its initial round of cases, the Accountability Program investigated whether companies were correctly and reliably providing consumers with an effective choice mechanism. Cases involved defective links to opt-out mechanisms and transparency that was deficient or otherwise lacking.

The DMA's enforcement program likewise builds on a long history of proactive and robust self-regulatory oversight. The DMA's longstanding Guidelines for Ethical Business Practice ("Guidelines") set out comprehensive standards for marketing practices, which all DMA members must follow as a condition of membership. The DAA Self-Regulatory Principles are incorporated into these Guidelines.

The DMA's Committee on Ethical Business Practice examines practices that may violate DMA Guidelines. To date, the DMA Guidelines have been applied to hundreds of marketing cases on a variety of issues such as deception, unfair business practices, personal information protection, and online behavioral advertising. In order to educate marketing professionals on acceptable marketing practices, a case report is regularly issued which summarizes questioned direct marketing promotions and how cases were administered. The report also is used to educate regulators and others interested in consumer protection issues about the DMA Guidelines and how they are implemented.

The Committee on Ethical Business Practice works with both member and non-member companies to gain voluntary cooperation in adhering to the guidelines and to increase good business practices for direct marketers. The DMA Corporate Responsibility team and Ethics Committee receive matters for review in a number of ways: from consumers; member companies; nonmembers; or, sometimes, consumer protection agencies. Complaints are reviewed against the Guidelines and Committee members determine how to proceed. If a potential violation is found to exist, the company will be contacted and advised on how it can come into full compliance.

Most companies work with the Committee to cease or change the questioned practice. However, if a member company does not cooperate and the Committee believes there are ongoing Guidelines violations, the Committee can recommend that action be taken by the Board of Directors and can make case results public. Board action could include censure, suspension or expulsion from membership, and the Board may also make its actions public. If a non-member or a member company does not cooperate and the Committee believes violations of law may also have occurred, the case is referred to federal and/or state law enforcement authorities for review.

The CBBB and DMA programs demonstrate the success of self-regulation and its many benefits, including the ability for the regulatory apparatus to evolve to meet new challenges. Importantly, accountability under the Principles applies to all members of the advertising ecosystem, not merely "members" of the various organizations.

End Notes

[1] Professor John Deighton, Harvard Business School, Economic Value of the Advertising-Supported Internet Ecosystem, at 81 (September 2012), available at http://www.iab.net/media/file/iab_Report_September-24- 2012_4clr_v1.pdf (last visited May 12, 2014).

[2] Id. at 66.

[3] Interactive Advertising Bureau 2013 Internet Advertising Report (April 2014) (reporting results of PricewaterhouseCoopers study), available at http://www.iab.net/AdRevenueReport (last visited on May 12, 2014).

[4] Interactive Survey of U.S. Adults commissioned by the DAA (April 2013), available at http://www.aboutads.info/DAA-Zogby-Poll.

[5] NAI Enforcement Page (providing Compliance Reports from 2009-2013), available at http://www.networkadvertising.org/code-enforcement/enforcement.

INDEX

D

E

Q

R

S